UNS

Chapter One
SAY CHEESE

1970's London

The top half of my body including my head is inside a cardboard wedge. It's like snorkelling; you can hear your own breath reverberating.
I've got this promotion job as a wedge of cheese. Double Gloucester. The woman to my left is Cheddar and next to her is Red Leicester. When they said promotional work, I presumed it would be handing out leaflets dressed up in the usual bimbo stuff: white high heels, Ra-Ra skirt and a clingy T-shirt with something inane like 'Say Cheese' scrawled across the chest. I never thought I'd actually be the stuff. The wedge is made of hardened cardboard with two holes drilled in it for your eyes, but they'd stuck netting over them like a pantomime horse, so everything's a blur and, if you need to look at something which isn't directly in front of you, the whole wedge has to turn. That's why I keep banging into things and knocking people over. They'd cut a slit like a slice of melon for a mouth and a couple of extra holes by the ear so we didn't suffocate. Thoughtful. My legs, in black tights, hang out the bottom

like those liquorice shoelaces you can buy at Woollies - all thin and weedy - and made to look even more thin and weedy by the Doc Martins on my feet. They are the finishing touch, along with the white gloves. I look - we all look - completely ridiculous, like one of those cartoons. I suppose that's the idea. The wedge itself is hot, heavy, smelly and awkward and God forbid you give vent to a burp. As for going to the loo -that's a day's work in itself. Someone had a laugh designing this. Must've been a man.

I've been thinking about them a lot lately. I just can't get it into my head how they've ended up on top for so many hundreds of years and how women have ended up like my Mum, a servant. How did that happen? After all, when we first started to develop, right at the beginning of our evolution, there wasn't anything in it, surely? We'd all have been running around grunting and feeding, except for the females who had babies, which you'd think was one up on men. I did history O and A Level and, although we'd learnt about 'The impact of the Corn Laws in the 17th Century', or 'Enclosure in the Highlands and the diaspora of the Scots in the 18th Century', we never touched on 'How women got shat on by men from the year Dot'.

For some reason, all the women in my extended family think men are the best. My mother even wanted to be one; she says she doesn't get on with women. Judging from her useless marriages, she didn't get on too well with men either, but it's obvious to me that she thinks James, my brother, is the bee's knees and I'm an 'also ran'. That pisses me off quite a bit because James has never lifted a finger to help Mum. It has always been me and, right now, I'm trying my best to make money so I can get her out of the impoverished situation she's in, along with me trying to get work as an actress. Problem is, I can barely make enough money to keep myself alive, never mind sustain her.

I'm envious of my friends because they never have to consider their parents. They can just swan off and do exactly what they like; go home every now and then and have a slap-up Sunday lunch, play with the family dog and sleep in the bedroom that's been embalmed for them to come back to years without end. It's not that important to them that they become rich and famous as it is for me because, if I don't, I won't be able to save my mother. That aside, I am going to make a point of finding out how women like my mother idolised men and despised themselves.

It's not that I hate men, apart from my stepfather, who thankfully is dead, but how is it that the wrong people, just because they were blokes, got to run everything to their advantage and why - despite the suffragettes - WHY women allowed themselves to get into such a sorry state from the get-go. I mean WHY?

I've discovered this place off St Martins Lane that has all these amazing, weird and wonderful bookshops with esoteric and feminist stuff that might have the answer, so I'm going there as soon as this job is over - if I survive it. I suppose there's something to be said for being banged up in a cardboard box all day; it gives you the opportunity to cogitate about stuff.

"Will you come outside with me? I'm so hot I think I'm going to faint." Red Leicester's whining on again. Now she's a case in point. She's one of those spineless girls who complain about everything and suck up to the boss so she can get all the plum jobs. I don't know how she does it - he's 40, if he's a day, with almost no hair. One of those thigh-chafing, sweaty-testicled salesmen who drive around the country in a Ford Fiesta going to exhibitions, staying in hotels and getting spliced in the bar at night, on the pull.

"HONESTLY?" I question. "You're HONESTLY going to faint?"

"Yes," comes the muffled reply. "I'm burning up in here. Please?"

"OK. But we'd better make it quick because you know what they're like if they catch us. They'll dock our pay and report us to the office and I need to get as much work as I can right now."

The piece of Cheddar comes too - safety in slices - but not for the punters. Three large triangles of cheese who can barely see where they're going, lumbering towards you down the narrow walkways must be a bit unnerving, especially as there's every danger of being speared on the thin end of a wedge. I catch sight of another poor bugger bouncing along as an orange. Apparently, he was working at the RSC last week. At least he's had a decent job. I've spent the last few weeks as a Barbie doll, a human fruit machine, another doll that smelled of synthetic strawberries and someone from outer space in what the designer thought was a futuristic jumpsuit. The suit was made out of something like Bacofoil and, in the hot July sunshine, as we pounded up and down Regent Street dispensing leaflets, it acted like a self-baster. My colleague ended up with such a severe dose of thrush, she could have opened a tofu factory. I lost about 4 pounds in weight.

"Do you want a fag?" Cheddar asks as she pulls a crumpled pack of ten from her sleeve.

"No thanks."

"Would you mind?"

"Oh, yeah, give it to me." I jam the ciggy as far as I can through her slit of a mouth so her lips can reach and light it for her. She stands there, a piece of cheese puffing away.

"Smoked cheddar, that's what you are," says Red Leicester who nearly kills herself laughing. It must be nice to be that simple. I watch her wedge heaving with mirth. And then I catch sight of old Baldy with the fat thighs.

"Shit! The boss is over there. Quick, run." We all take off at once. I can hear Cheddar shouting, "My fag! My fag! I'm going to burn!" Too bad. I'm away. It's not easy running in this get-up, in fact, it's almost impossible. The whole thing is bouncing up and down, banging the top of my head, and I can hear my breath going in and out like I'm on a ventilator. I see Red Leicester ahead of me making for the main door, but there's a queue. Panicking, I take a chance and head for the revolving one. Big mistake. It sucks me in and drags me round by the snout. And round and round and round. The thing is relentless as people feed themselves through. I'm desperately trying to stay upright, shouting, "Help! Stop it! Stop it! Help!"

Finally, I manage to jerk the wedge free and throw myself out and I'm sent spinning into the crowds. I manage to stagger for a few paces screaming, "Mind out! Get out of the way!" My white-gloved hands wave frantically, but gravity proves too much and I'm sent crashing to the floor, landing on my back like an overturned turtle. Christ, how humiliating. "I'm down! Help me, I'm down! Can someone help me? I can't get up. Please. Someone...?"

"OK, I've got you. 'Ere grab her other hand. That's it, upsa daisy."

I'm pulled to my feet by two salesmen from the microwave stand. "Thanks very much," I say, tottering to one side as I try to get my balance.

"I think your friend's in trouble over there," says one of the men, openly guffawing. I angle myself around to see Red Leicester stuck in the doorway, the boss trying to wrench her out. No sign of 'smoked Cheddar'. She may well be by now. I turn away. I'm not hanging around. I can't afford to lose this job. I shuffle off into the crowds, biffing people with the crumpled end of my wedge as I go, "Sorry/excuse me/sorry."

Chapter Two
THE TOMB

I'm going down to the countryside to see Mum. I'm driving down in my new battered old car my friend gave me. It's been in a prang so the front is a 2CV and the back is a Citroën Dyane. It's completely hideous. All the paintwork has lost its shine and one part is blue and the other is red, but it was free as it failed its M.O.T. Luckily, I found this little Greek guy in Clapham to get it going. Ulysses Apostiladese was his name. With a name like that, l knew he'd sort it. My car may be ugly, but she's brilliant and I love her. I call her Saf. That's her number plate. If you run out of oil in a 2CV, you just mash up some bananas and they'll keep going in a desert. Fact.

I tried her out on the motorway the other day. She was a bit slow but I found, if I tucked in behind lorries, I was carried along in their slipstream. At one point, I got up to 75 miles an hour, but she started to shake and I thought she was in danger of disintegrating. I could see myself going down the motorway with bits dropping off until it was just a steering wheel, some tyres and me, like Buster Keaton in one of those old silent movies.

I don't want to go and see Mum. Not because I don't love her, but because her situation never gets any better, which is frustrating and really sad. She is still being moved on every year or so to some god-forsaken hovel in exchange for another menial job. They say money doesn't make you happy. People talk a load of shit. I would rather be miserable rich than miserable poor. I worked out that, in the 17 years I spent with Mum and my brothers, we had moved 21 times! One of which was a 2-room barn with no loo. Bucket in the hedge sort of thing. Luckily, I'd escaped the humiliation of living in someone's garden shed as I had my first job by then, but poor Boney, my younger brother, didn't. Nevertheless, the image of the wasps' nest, like a chandelier hanging over Mum's camp bed, remains photographically in my memory.

I'm dreading this visit more than most as we are going to see horrid Granny (her mother). No one likes Granny but she's old and widowed so you have to be tolerant. She and Grandfather stuck James and I in the orphanage so, as I see it, I don't owe her much in the way of compassion.

Granny lives in this great big Gothic mansion in the woods, where she has her own rooms. It's a private retirement place for 'People Like Us', as she calls them. It costs an arm and a leg so that's why she can't help Mum out - or so she says, but she wouldn't anyway. She treats her two daughters like something out of a Dostoevsky novel, setting them against each other with the promise of great things in her will; telling each one privately how she prefers one more than the other; the old British Empire strategy of Divide and Conquer.

Coming off the motorway, I turn onto the old familiar B roads. The countryside always looks sad to me now, like an old friend I've nothing left in common with. It used to mean so much; the hedgerows, woods and spinneys; the fold of the fields, smell of cowpats, gold of dandelions, froth of cow parsley. With each plant, the months known to me as they came blossoming, burgeoning and dying with the seasons. It felt as much a part of me as my breath, but I've turned my back on it since I moved to live in London. I feel guilty, as if I have betrayed the thing that nurtured me, but at the same time, it makes me angry. I want to step into different worlds, experience a different kind of life and fix my mum so I can be released.

I come off the B road and bump down a long drive through woods that give way to dark green bushes of rhododendrons on either side, then over a small stone bridge and there, rising up in the gloom, the imposing Victorian pile stares blankly out. I recognise Mum's equally battered old car and catch sight of her being ushered in through the large medieval oak door by Mr Dubchek, the Polish caretaker. "Wait for me," I shout as I park up and scrabble to collect my things.

Stepping into the spacious wood-panelled hall, I give Mum a hug. "Hello, Mr Dubchek," I say. He nods at me, unsmiling. He looks like one of the Addams Family; heavy, putty-coloured face with dark-ringed eyes that tell a tale of sleepless nights. He steps behind us, closing the door with an echoing clunk, then, with another nod, turns and disappears down a dark corridor.

"It's the war you know. The Poles suffered dreadfully." Mum whispers as we climb the stairs of the grand central staircase which rises up and curls off to left and right at the first floor. We pad down the heavily carpeted hallway to Granny's room encased in its silence. Old age always seems to be silent, silent and dusty.

Granny is pretty ancient but dignified. She always dresses well - muted classics, cashmere, jade earrings, pearls and tweed. She is delicate, small, upright and imperious but her smile comes easily, unexpectedly and is disarming. Her skin is very soft and she has THE most aristocratic nose in the whole world. It is sublime. Not one of us inherited it. In fact, our side of the family has inherited very little from her – not the skin, the eyes, the nose, – not even her sociopathic behaviour which, let's face it, in this day and age is a must. Actually, I lie; I think Mum and I got her dodgy hormones and of course Mum got her endless derision and criticism; her generosity there was unmatched. The unfortunate thing about Granny though is her wobbly head, which reminds me of those nodding dogs people put in the back of their cars. It hasn't always wobbled, of course, it's something that has come with age.

We sit and sip our China tea out of paper-thin bone china cups. I struggle to choke back a dreaded fish-paste sandwich. It's like cat food. Why on earth does Granny like it?

Conversation is like an old car running out of petrol, hiccoughing its way down a dead end, dying out momentarily, then kick-starting again to judder along for a few sentences before spluttering to a full stop. There isn't a lot to talk about - or rather there is so much that it would blow the room apart, as Mum sits on her years of accumulated hurt and fury with tightened buttocks.

"Are you still playing bridge with Gwyneth?" she asks, scratching around for something to talk about which doesn't have a lit fuse attached to it.

"Gwyneth?" echoes Granny, head shaking from side to side.

"Yes, Gwyneth. That's who you partner with isn't it?"

"Don't be silly," Granny replies with a twist of a smile. "She fell off her perch a week ago."

"Oh. That's a shame. You didn't tell me."

"No, well, what's to tell? There isn't a week that goes by without one or another dropping down dead."

"I thought you rather liked her," continues Mum.

"Like?" snorts Granny. "She called the lavatory the toilet and the sitting room a lounge. Living here, you don't meet people you like, you meet people you can bear. After all, beggars can't be choosers." Mum looks down at her cup avoiding Granny's pleading stare.

Out of politeness, Granny turns to me. "Darling, what are you up to these days? Any auditions?"

"Erm, well, no. Right now, I'm doing this and that. Promotional work. That sort of thing."

"I thought Mummy said you were working in an all-night chemist. Am I wrong?"

Mum shoots me a warning glance. The so-called all-night chemist is in fact a sex shop. "Oh, yes… but part-time only," I lie.

"Ah." She looks hungrily back at Mum like a dog waiting for a treat. She looks to her, hoping for some kindness, some lightheartedness, because Granny likes a joke when she's not condemning the world's inhabitants for everything. Always a party girl, her long-term sugar daddy, 'Uncle Anthony' so-called, who was very rich, kept her on holidays and other necessities. From Grandfather's point of view, he may well have been viewed as an investment that paid good dividends in exchange for being cuckolded year after year. The truth is, 'Uncle Anthony' more or less kept them all alive at times. Poor Grandfather, being a 'gentleman' meant that work was out of the question since he'd lost all his lands and money with the demise of his first marriage when he seduced my grandmother and got her pregnant. Another one tripped up by his cock.

A strangled pause is interrupted by the peacocks wailing on the lawn outside. I catch sight of the old leather travel alarm clock ticking by the bedside table. Next to it, a bottle of pills throws its shadow across the polish of the mahogany. The dark interior of the room seems to be eating Granny up, nibbling away until there's nothing left or just enough left for us, her family, to cremate. "Well, we have to make a move." Mum rises up.

Granny, nodding ever more frantically, looks up at her with a desperate expression. "Oh, must you, darling? So soon?" she pleads, struggling to her feet.

"Yes, I can't sit around all day. I have got to get back as the Mostrams are having a group down for the weekend and I have to get everything ready."

"I'm so sorry you have to do this sort of work."

"So am I," Mum replies curtly and I look at Granny, willing her to pull out her chequebook to write a cheque for thousands so Mum will never have to skivvy and cook again. She doesn't of course.

When we take our leave, I notice Mum's expression soften. Guilt and compassion replace bitterness and anger. We both know we are about to shut the tomb door on a person who no longer has the power of vibrant life and she's frightened. I think to myself, 'she should have thought of that when she was handing it out."

As we walk away down the hall, I keep saying to myself, "She's a bitch, she's a bitch, you know she's a bitch. She's just an old bitch now, that's all but she's still a bitch... with a wobbly head." That last bit about the head makes me feel guilty all over again.

Mum gets in the car and leans out the window. "Thank God that's over for another week."

The dreadful thing is, I almost feel the same when I leave Mum. But it's longer than a week before I see her again, it's as long as I can stretch it out.

Chapter Three
GRANNY (AND I) TAKE A TRIP

My quest for 'where did it all go wrong for women' is on the march. I'd managed to find a bookshop in St Martin's Court full of esoteric stuff along with books on women's history.

It turns out that the penis first appeared in the Age of the Reptiles (surprise, surprise) about 200 million years ago. I had no idea. One doesn't really think of the penis having a history all to itself. I have to say, it's a horrid name that. It's nearly as bad as 'scrotum', which sounds like an offshoot of the disease Scrofula, which interestingly results in bulbous swellings too – though at the other end of the body. In any case, back to the history lesson. We women were mostly managing on our own until we became landlubbers and that's when the willy came in - or rather came out. The body of a female was a safer place for eggs to develop, hidden away. What interests me most is witchcraft and witches. I'm not talking hocus pocus, black cats and women whizzing around on broomsticks with boils all over their faces, but the real role women played as witches; why they were denigrated, why the name 'witch' became associated with everything evil. 'Witch' meant 'wise woman' in old parlance, but no one seemed to remember that, at least not since men started getting paranoid and began torturing them. I often wonder why men were/are so frightened of women having any sort of power. When we ran away from my stepfather, Mum couldn't get a loan or anything unless he gave permission to the bank manager. Can you believe it? I mean, as if he would to his runaway wife! Anyhow, I've gone one step further and found someone who is actually a practising witch running courses on how to be one, somewhere in Tooting. I start next Tuesday. I can't wait.

I'm not going to tell my boyfriend as he'll just take the piss. Talking of which, I don't think I can live with him much longer. Bedtime is getting more and more impossible. I know if I stayed with him, I'd be safe and I'm aware arranged marriages can be quite successful in some ways, but that's mostly about breeding and hanging on to money. I won't be doing any of that. I'll never marry and I am certainly never going to have kids. The mere thought of having something living in my body, feeding off me, makes me feel revolted. After all, that's what tapeworms do, don't they? I tend to keep that observation to myself or I just appear to be weirder than I already think people think I am. Obviously, a baby is very different from a tapeworm, but that's what it felt like to me when I got pregnant a couple of years ago. My hormones were dancing this peculiar kind of psychotic jig and I thought I was going round the bend. Much longer like that and I would have been sectioned. As it was, I'd decided to have an abortion. God, don't people just jump up and down when you use that word? The odd thing is that only a few years before, women couldn't have an abortion unless they were mad. I had to impress on the doctor I wasn't, but actually, I sort of was. I never told anyone because people thought you were a monster or a tart. What's monstrous, to my way of thinking, is having kids when you are a psychopath like my stepfather. As for being a tart, this wasn't the result of a one-night stand. It was the result of not being able to take the pill and a useless condom.

It was early one bleak February morning when I took the tube to the end of the Bakerloo line - which I threw up on as I had morning sickness. The other passengers of which, thankfully, there were only a couple, had to sit with me and IT for at least 6 stops because I had nothing to clear IT up with. No one said anything, they just stared at me in horror then turned away, holding down their own breakfasts. The sordidness of the whole situation was unbelievably shaming and, worse still, I started crying, but I think that was just my crazy hormones making me do that. I found the place with my A-Z - a 10-minute walk from the station. The Victorian house was clean and clinical with other shame-faced-looking women sitting in a line of chairs in the hallway. I sat down next to a young woman with bare, white legs. They were very white. We didn't chat. What would you say? "Come here often?"

I was in and out quite quickly. It wasn't nice; very painful cramps afterwards, which doubled me up, but that was to be expected. I felt so guilty and angry with myself that I accepted them as a sort of punishment. I got a taxi all the way home, which was a real luxury, and it took all my money, but I had to. The only downside was that I got an infection, but no sense of loss; nothing, only relief. I can't work out if it's because I am just not maternal or whether it's because I was brought up to think children are the ruination of all your hopes and dreams and should be avoided at all costs. I don't know. It's the old nature/nurture thing, isn't it? Bit of both, I suspect. I love animals and my mum of course and on and off, deep down, my brothers, I suppose. Oh, and Dad, but I don't see much of him now. I'm just not a human baby person. All that Mother Nature stuff really isn't my bag. Watching any sort of childbirth on the telly, even if it's a cow or a sheep, really makes me squirm. All these people going, "Ah, isn't it amazing! It's a miracle," while I'm frozen to the sofa thinking, 'This is unbelievably repulsive'. The sheer, slimy pink and red of it all makes me shudder. Thank God we weren't all born inside out.

The best news. I've got a job dressed up as a female Lawrence of Arabia riding a camel in an advert for rice. I should earn a reasonable amount of dosh doing that, so I will be able to pay Mum's garage bill and take her out. Maybe this is it. Maybe at last I'm turning a corner and my luck has changed.

Meanwhile, I had my first meeting at the witch's house. It took some finding as it was in a Tooting backwater amongst a parade of shops with the windows blacked out. The front door opened straight into the main living area, which was jammed with books from floor to ceiling. It had that feel of the 'intellectual shabby' that I had come across in North London. Well-to-do middle-class artistic types who had houses and apartments in Belsize Park or Camden that smelled of earthy food, sunshine on dusty books, wood smoke from a fire with a splash of patchouli. These folk weren't well off like those and their place differed in that it had an underlying niff of unclean. Not cockroach heaven, but close. If the beasties hadn't set up camp there already, I could see them moving in within a couple of weeks unless someone got the hoover out. I nearly trod on an ugly toddler with a wonky eye called Merlin who was crawling around on the filthy floor. I looked at him thinking he must be pretty tough to have survived the dirt but then, of course he would be; he was a wizard.

Quite an assortment of people, all jostled for a place in the cramped space whilst several cats, unperturbed by the swarm of would-be witches, draped themselves on piles of books and looked on impassively. By the fireplace, slumped in a raggedy chair, sat Rumplestiltskin, his nose in a book. He turned out to be the husband and worked for that den of Marxism, Lambeth Council.

Our teacher, who was a big woman in her thirties with long, black hair, had obviously dressed for the occasion, donning a black satin floor-length dress. It turned out she had a degree in Theology and was the daughter of a vicar. Bet there were some ugly scenes around the dinner table at the family home when she came out as a witch; maybe her dad excommunicated her or simply hung some garlic on the front door. "Hello everyone. Help yourself to tea and herbals. Leave your course money in the box on the side and, when we are all here, we will go through to the back." Refusing the offer of tea (I noticed that the kitchen tops were pretty much the same state as the carpet), I paid my 6 quid and tried not to feel disappointed by the look of my fellow students. The toddler was scooped up, wailing, dumped on the lap of Rumple, and we were guided out into the small garden at the back to a circular wooden hut.

It was dark and warm inside with big cushions all the way round the perimeter and a makeshift 'altar' in the middle with candles and a pot, otherwise known as a cauldron. I sat next to a pretty woman on one side, who told me she did 'spiritual dancing' and on the other, a jittery young man dressed in black who looked a bit like a rubber Gonk I was once given for Christmas when I was 9.

Our Tuesday evenings consisted of learning about the history of the 'Old Religion' (i.e. Paganism), how to cast a circle, keeping the Sabbaths, why witches had been persecuted; Christianity and its effect on the status of women, Alastair Crowley (maniac,), Covens (careful), hedge witches (care in the community) and finally her own particular form of witchcraft that she referred to as the 'Craft'. She passed around the book that she'd published about her experiences and everyone pretended not to ogle the 'sky clad', i.e. starkers photos of herself doing some ritual or another. It took quite a while getting back to her because you know what women are like - always interested in seeing other women's flabby bits. She also passed around her meditation drum which was handmade and which, she told us proudly, she had decorated using her own menstrual blood. I'd wondered what the browny-coloured bits were on the parchment. I thought that was pretty revolting; bad enough having a period without smearing it all over a musical instrument. It was that 'natural' thing again. Anyway, there's almost nothing 'natural' about me. I always wear make-up and streak my hair so now I'm blonde not 'natural' mouse brown. In fact, I use any artifice I can to get me away from what I actually look like.

It was some weeks into the course when we were asked if we wanted to go at the weekend to help save some woods. "If you can all make it, the more power we will have to protect the sacred area," cajoled our head witch. "The trees are our oldest friends. We need them. We must stand by and defend them with our collective power." Part of me wanted to believe that we had this extraordinary power, but the greater part of me feared we would be more like characters out of a sitcom.

Since the woods were out Norwood way, I didn't have to worry about bumping into anyone I knew. I mean Norwood! "Where the hell is that?" I asked the dancing girl, whose name I discovered had been Shirley and had now changed it to Aeone. As luck would have it, she lived nearby so I agreed to pick her up and she'd direct me. Turned out she lived with a fruitarian who was a yoga master. I sort of knew she would.

I drew up outside her place, expecting it to be a bit of a squat, because goodness knows there wasn't much money to be made in spiritual dancing, especially since she only did it when the mood took her and usually to random members of the unsuspecting public along her scruffy high street.

Sure enough, the house appeared pretty run down. It was one in a street of 1920s semis that seemed to stretch forever. The front garden had a whole lot of junk in it and the flaking neon pink paint on the front door added to the general shabbiness. I rang the doorbell and was surprised to hear it worked. When she opened the door and asked me in, I was about to say I'd wait in the car, thinking it might be similarly unhygienic to the witch's place, but was pleasantly surprised to see white wall-to-wall carpeting. At the end of the white corridor, a shaft of orange light streamed through a half-open door. "Wow!" I exclaimed. "What's going on in there?"

"The kitchen. Go and have a look around whilst I get myself together," she replied. I headed towards the glow.

The whole room was illuminated with what seemed like a golden, almost spiritual, light. Its provenance was an orange gel covering the windows so that, when light hit from outside, the place was bathed in Costa del Sol-style sunlight. The room itself wasn't very big but it had a stream of water running around it, about a foot from the edge, like a small moat. Stepping stones enabled you to get from one side to the other, stopping on the way to rest on a small mound, which I suppose was designed for someone to sit and eat. I crossed the stream to the far side where a gnarled tree trunk rose up through the floor, one branch disappearing out through the wall. Carefully built into its side was the tiniest fully functioning cooker. When I say 'tiny', I mean suitable for a small elf. Around the rest of the room hung small cupboards which opened this way and that, defying any logical presumptions. I wondered if, when you staggered down in the morning after a hard night, this might be a problem as you'd forget the landscape and fall into the stream, bludgeoning yourself on the edges of the doors as you fumbled to open them the right way. Given the size of the cooker, a fry-up would have taken all day, but then you don't usually fry fruit. "Wow," I said again as I made my way back down the hall. "That is amazing."

"Go upstairs if you want. Just need to go to the loo then I'll be ready."

I climbed the stairs onto the landing where I saw, cut into the wall, a very small door with a key hanging by it. Couldn't see a bottle saying 'Drink me'. As it wasn't locked, I squeezed through and almost banged my head on the construction inside that filled the whole room. It was the shape of a dodecahedron made out of what seemed to be white paper but more robust. I was about to open one of the hinged segments to crawl in when I heard something scuffling inside, like an alarmed rodent. I paused for a moment, then I heard a grunt so I was pretty sure it must have been the yoga man and, since she'd told me he was an anti-social Scorpio, I quickly withdrew. I was about to head off down the landing to see what the bathroom was like when she called up, "Ready."

We met up with the other pagans and held the tree blessing ceremony which was somewhat mundane after her place. Being chilly, no one went 'sky-clad' - thankfully. We chanted a bit and meditated a bit and then went to the pub for a beer.

It was nearing the end of the course when we were invited to do a process called pathworking. "What's that about?" I asked.

"Oh, it's amazing. It's like therapy," enthused Aeone.

"None of that primal screaming stuff I hope," I replied nervously.

"No. It's like an adventure story. The way you respond to the experiences in the story often resonates within your own life, which gives you insight into what you need to look at."

That sounded quite interesting and we had a perfect evening for it, the weather cold with a biting wind outside as we gathered in the warmth of the wooden hut. The fire and candles were lit in preparation so the room was lovely and cosy – dirty, but cosy. Relaxing back on the old cushions and closing our eyes, our head witch started us off on our journey.

"You are standing in front of four massive oak doors. One to the west, one to the east, one to the north and one to the south. Which door do you choose? You pause and then walk towards the south. As you lift your hands to the door, it opens and you walk through. You find yourself high up on an escarpment, looking down on a valley which stretches far, far away to the horizon." So, the adventure began. She took us scrambling up ice-covered mountains, strolling through meadows, forging torrents, wading through stagnant water, staggering through burning deserts and dawdling in cool woods.

Each place had its own particular challenge followed by a bit of a lull. I have to say I was quite enjoying it until it came to the bit where we found ourselves being sent down into the underworld. "We walk into a dark cave where a woman presses two silver coins into our hands and points us toward a tunnel. The coins are to pay the ferryman who will take us across the river. We drag ourselves on our fronts down an increasingly narrow tunnel with water trickling down on either side. The smell of damp pervades the air and the feel of mould-covered stones underneath makes it difficult to pull ourselves along. It's freezing cold and it seems like it's never going to end."

Yeah, I would have skipped a few pages here and I was just thinking, 'maybe I might just open my eyes and have a squint at the others', when our witch said, "Finally, we stop in a place where we can stretch our limbs and rest for a moment and, as we do, we hear the sound of running water. A few more paces and it opens up into a huge cave lit by torches with a river, cold and black, flowing through it. The river Styx. Standing by a boat tied to a post on the bank, is a man with his back to us. Surrounding him is a throng of shadowy figures, their hands held out as if pleading with him, the expressions on their withered faces, desperate and woeful. They are the ghosts of those who can never cross the river to the land of the dead. They are the undead. The man turns and, seeing us, walks towards us. The wraiths follow him, pulling and plucking at him, but their hands pass straight through him. As he approaches us, we hold out our hands with the silver coins, our payment to cross the river. The wraiths, seeing this, rush at us. We must stand our ground and not be fearful."

Now this was where it all went very weird for me. I could see myself waiting in turn for the ferryman. I didn't like being there and was keen to get on the boat and leave. It wasn't nice to know these people would never find peace and it made me feel uncomfortable, but there was nothing I could do. Suddenly, out of the ghostly throng, a face loomed up in front of me. It wasn't weeping and moaning like the rest. It was smiling.

It was Duncan.

Duncan, my dead stepfather.

He looked at the coins in my hand then thrust out his hand. I backed away. The smile vanished and a look of fury overtook it. Suddenly, his mouth opened wide as his head cracked to one side then fell back, letting out a soundless scream. Shit! I sat up and opened my eyes. My teacher looked at me enquiringly. "Sorry, need to... erm... need to stretch my legs?" I mouthed and went outside and quickly lit up a fag. What the hell was that? I hadn't thought of Duncan for ages. Even Mum didn't mention him now, at least, not in front of me.

"Are you alright?" I looked up to see our teacher padding towards me across the scrubby wet grass in her bare feet, miraculously avoiding the cat shit speckling her pathway.

"Oh, yes. Fine."

She checked me out for a couple of seconds without saying anything, like she was trying to see deep into my mind. I had to turn away, pretending I found the brick wall opposite really fascinating. "You know, pathworking can be very powerful at times. It can bring up a lot of stuff to the surface from your subconscious, sometimes things that haven't been dealt with that need looking at, things you haven't come to terms with. It's very cleansing."

I nodded. "Yeah, I'm sure. Yeah, it's really good. Really interesting... I just got a bit of cramp in my leg, that's all. I get it sometimes." She gave me a funny look like, 'Are you sure about that?' I smiled and took another puff before dogging out my fag on the ground. "Actually, I don't feel too hot. Didn't sleep well last night. Maybe I'll go home early tonight."

"Sure?" She gave me one of those, 'I don't believe you' sort of looks, but I just faced her out. I wasn't telling her anything. I don't tell anybody anything about my family.

"Sure," I smiled back. I followed her into the hut, grabbed my things and slunk off back through the house, past Rumplestiltskin slumped in the raggedy armchair by the fire with the ubiquitous book, the toddler asleep at his feet. "Bye," I mumbled, not waiting for a reply as I headed for the door and quickly let myself out. It had started to rain.

As I trundled back home in Saf, I tried hard to erase the image of Duncan's screaming face bubbling up in the watery blur of headlights of the oncoming traffic. Pathworking, I decided, was out for the time being if it meant he was going to pop up.

"Anyway," I muttered to myself. "Whatever were we all doing going on a boat trip to Hades like a bunch of tourists? We are the living. We shouldn't be visiting places like that."

We shouldn't be, but it turned out Granny just had.

"How did she do it?" I asked.

Mum sounded strangely cold. "She gave the maid some money to buy her a bottle of brandy, then she got in the bath with her slip on, and took the pills with the brandy."

I stared at the wall in front of me, the telephone pressed to my ear, and tried to imagine what that would have felt like; the day you wake up and make the decision, the moment you sit down and write the letter, running the bath – how deep should it be? Opening the drawer and deciding for the last time which slip to wear, which pair of knickers; the moment you climb into the bath, the warm water surging round your body for the last time as you lower yourself in - everything – everything, for the last time.

The feel of the pills in your mouth.

Swig from the bottle.

Swallow.

No going back.

"She wrote in her letter that she'd killed herself because her daughters didn't care for her," Mum's voice cut through, brittle with anger. "Both the policeman and maid had read it before I got there and they looked at me like I was a murderer. They all did."

"Oh, Mum."

"All my life, she did nothing but put me down - criticise me. Even in death, she had to punish me."

I didn't know what to say so I said, "Oh, Mum," again.

"I have to go now. I have to get everything sorted out. The Dubceks want her room."

"I'll come down and help," I offered, dreading the idea. "I can be there by about eleven tomorrow morning."

"You don't have to do that. Probably best if I just get on with it by myself."

"No, Mum. I want to help."

"Alright," she sighed and I could hear the anger dissipate as weariness took over. "I'd better go."

I sat staring at the wall for ages thinking about Granny. Then, I remembered when Mum asked me if I'd mind if she committed suicide. It was around the anniversary of Duncan's death. She was quite calm and we'd had a nice day together. I'd bought two cream-filled meringues for our tea as a treat and she said, "Darling, I want to ask you something. How would you feel if I came to a point where I just had had enough and wanted to die? Would you understand if I committed suicide?" She had this soft sort of apologetic smile on her face at the time. I felt my stomach do a sickening flip. I immediately thought, 'Now, keep calm. Don't let on you're freaked out. Think of her,' because this wasn't a hypothetical question.

I gave myself a moment and then, with a sort of contemplative sigh, said, absolutely normally, "Well, it wouldn't make me happy. In fact, it would be pretty difficult; but if you felt so miserable that you really didn't think you could carry on Mum, then I would have to deal with it. After all, it's not about me, is it?" Even though what I wanted to say – no, I wanted to scream, – 'For fuck's sake, have you any idea what that would to me? Kill yourself - are you fucking mad? It would crucify me. Please don't do this!' But I didn't, because I believe that, when you really love someone, you don't think of yourself first, you think of the other person. The weird thing is, Mum looked almost disappointed with my reply.

Thinking of Granny again, I wondered if she'd managed to pay the ferryman - or if she'd joined the wraiths. I cheered myself up a bit with the Pagan idea of reincarnation. Not if you'd had a shit life and you'd got to embark on another obviously, but if Granny could come back as a dog for instance, she might learn to be nicer. As a dog, she'd love her master/mistress unconditionally like dogs do, with no thought for themselves. Maybe a few dog lives and after that, she could have another crack at being a human being – but no kids. No kids until she'd had a few more reincarnations and could do the job properly.

I made myself a cup of tea and went into the bedroom and sat next to Big Ted, my old teddy bear. People scorn Ted like I'm a baby keeping my cuddly toys with me. Little do they know he holds the secrets of all my life. This bear was my link to my home whilst incarcerated in boarding school from the age of 7 and, when I go to burn, he will be coming too. Ted is a bit like religion. If you get to believe in it early enough, you never really let go. I know Ted isn't real but, somewhere in the denizens of my mind, there is something that says, 'What if?' Just like some of the God people I know. They don't really believe in Hell and angels or Christ rising up, but they hedge their bets because it's been imprinted from an early age - especially when they are about to cop it.

"Poor old Granny," I said out loud, because you know, however bad someone was, and after all, she wasn't Myra Hindley, you wouldn't want anyone to feel like she must have done. I could sense I was hitting a major downer. I needed someone to get me through it, someone who was relentlessly unforgiving.

I went round to see my brother James.

He was having one of his good days. He and his cat were in his marijuana room. It was like the hot house at Kew Gardens in there. He'd managed to rig up these special lights and blacked out the windows. His electricity bill must be massive though, knowing James, he wouldn't be paying for it. He'd probably draining some other unsuspecting resident's supply in the block.

"Now then my little chickens, what have we got here hmmm?" he cooed as he strapped up a heavily bushed plant that had lurched into its neighbour. There were rows and rows of these things, all neatly planted out in large pots. James tutted and clucked as he tended to their needs. He's always in a good frame of mind when he's nurturing them. I'd never seen him care for any other living thing the way he cares for the plants. Not even his cat - or the woman he lives with, who comes after the cat - but then the cat is something else. She is very beautiful.

He stopped by a particularly large plant and studied it with the love light in his eyes, letting out a sigh of admiration, shaking his head in wonderment. "Holy moly girl, you are finer than frog hair." He stroked a large leaf tenderly.

"Did you speak to Mum?" I asked. "Did she tell you about Granny?"

"Ssshhh! Not in here." He put his finger to his lips. "Don't want bad vibes in front of them." He nodded at the plants then motioned me towards the door. The cat padded after us.

We went into the sitting room with cups of instant coffee and sat by the window. James leaned back in his armchair, picking up his guitar. "Yup," he said, sucking air through his teeth and plucking idly on the strings. "Bad business. Bad business. But then, I knew it would be. All that hate." My brother reminded me more and more of Mr Micawber - on dope.

"Sad though, isn't it?" I said.

"She was a wicked old bat, Angela. Lest you forget, she kept us locked up in her kitchen garden day after day when we were only toddlers, then dumped us in the orphanage. Don't waste your sympathy on her. You reap what you sow and she had it coming to her. At least now she's dead, Mum might have a bit of money." He reached forward to grab himself a Black Jack chew out of a carton he kept by his chair. "Fucking families," he added as he popped one in and started sucking. "They piss me off."

I stared out of the window. The blossom on the blackthorn outside was just beginning to show.

The cat jumped up on my lap.

James played Bert Janchs' 'Angie' on the guitar.

I knew I could rely on James.

As it happened, Granny left very little. We overestimated her savings. But what she had, she'd left to Mum, not to her wealthy sister. Cunning old bag. It was only a tiny bit of money and some family silver. Mum could barely afford the 5th hand Skoda she'd had her eye on. Unfortunately, her sister, my aunt Maddie, despite being encrusted in dosh, didn't agree. So now they weren't talking – again! I took it back believing Granny should come back as a dog. She wouldn't be advanced enough for that. A sewer rat with mange was more the ticket.

Mum was very strange when I went down to help out. She hardly spoke as she sorted through Granny's clothes. I kept eyeing the door to the bathroom - the scene of the suicide - frightening myself with the thought that Granny's malevolent spirit was crouching in the bath, like some wizened harpy, waiting for us to walk in so she could tear us apart with her claws as she screamed her blame. "I don't want to go in the bathroom, Mum, if you don't mind," I said pathetically. She looked up at me from where she was kneeling, emptying a drawer full of underwear into a suitcase. She didn't reply.

"Sorry. Shall I see if I can get us some coffee?"

She nodded and looked back down at the small, neatly folded thermal vests in her hand. There was something sad and defenceless about small things. Mum was small. Granny was small.

"Right. It won't be long." I walked out of the room and turned to shut the door. As I did, I caught sight of Mum sitting motionless, staring at the vests. Then she did something that confused me. Holding them up, she buried her face in them, her body sagged as she let out a muffled whimper.

I pulled the door to and stood still in the echoing emptiness of the silent corridor.

Chapter Four
THE YEAR OF THE CAT

1970'S:

I have finally been to see a dentist about my teeth; my front ones especially. He's a friend of a friend so I felt I could trust him but, when I went for a consultation appointment, he said something about doing a filling there and then. I leapt out of the chair and said very loudly that I had already explained what a very bad time I'd had with dentists in the past and, if he attempted to even touch my gums, let alone my teeth, without sedation, I would scream. He looked a bit shocked and the nurse asked me to keep it down because they didn't want the people in the waiting room to hear, but he got the message. For today's appointment, he'd given me a pill to take last night before I went to sleep and then again one this morning and it's been marvellous. So far, I haven't felt a thing. I am not supposed to drive and he thinks someone is going to pick me up and take me home to sleep it off, but the trouble is, I've got an audition for a play. At last! I've parked my motorbike a street away and left my helmet with it so the dentist won't know.

All sorts of things would be good about getting this job. I'd be away from London, which means I would be away from the boyfriend and it could ease me out of the relationship without too much upset. You know 'out of sight out of mind/ What the eye don't see, the heart don't grieve over' and you never know, it might be the step I've been waiting for in terms of my career. This theatre has a really good reputation. I need to put my head down and get earning but, apart from needing the money, it would be so great to get famous enough to sit there in chat shows and tell everybody what you think about everything and how humble you are and how you just fell into it quite by mistake. That's what they all say. It's funny, they all make it appear so effortless - handpicked by fate.

"Right Angela," says the dentist from behind his surgical mask as he leans into me. He has very bushy eyebrows. "We are nearly there. I'm rewarded to find that, despite the colour of your teeth, you have kept them beautifully clean. Unlike some of my patients. Open wider please whilst I just push this into place... Yes," he continues. "I have one man who came to me with so much plaque on his teeth, I scraped it off and put it on a Jacobs cracker so he could see what it was like." I groan with revulsion and wave my hand in an effort to get him to stop but he ignores me. "I say one Jacobs cracker but there was enough from his upper teeth alone to cover three. I thought I should garnish them with a slice of gherkin and a cocktail onion just to get my point across. There now, that should do it. Have a rinse."

He's a bit weird this dentist but, once I see my temporary caps sparkling back at me in the mirror, I almost hug him. I give all the people in the waiting room a huge, anaesthetically lopsided smile, as I walk out. My teeth had been discoloured when I was a toddler by antibiotics saving me from pneumonia, but now, with pegs like these, I just know they are going to enhance my forthcoming audition. I'm planning on giving my rendition of feisty Kate from The Taming of the Shrew. Why, it's practically in the bag...

Bag it was, but how it got in there, I have no idea. The drugs obviously worked a treat. I have no recollection of what happened on that day apart from waking up at home at two in the morning, fully dressed. I had a brief interlude in the kitchen with some left-over Chinese, then back to bed, finally surfacing at 9.30 the next day. What happened in between is lost to the winds but obviously something good happened because apparently, I did the audish, got the job and am up here in the freezing cold north, ten days into rehearsals. I say something good, but I'm not so sure. I'm sitting here having breakfast at the B&B in my coat, hat and gloves, wiping the frost off my toast, adding anti-freeze to the tea. The mad woman who runs this place is obviously saving on bills and has one very small, old ceramic electric fire on half-power to warm the entire room. I suppose I shouldn't complain; compared to my icebox of a bedroom, this is like being on the rim of Vesuvius. I've hardly had any sleep due to the cold - and itching. I suspect her old black Labrador was using my bed to kip in before I arrived. When I pulled back the covers, there was a distinct black outline of a dog etched on the pink bobbly Brentford nylon sheets, like you see at a scene of a murder, so I'm sleeping with just the blankets. I should have said something at the time, but I was tired and it was late. Anyway, I don't want the aggro. I'll just move as soon as I have time to look for somewhere else.

Can't say I'm enjoying the job either; the director keeps picking on me and making snide comments about my dreadlocks which I had put in to look good for the band I was in back in London. They are amazing: long, blonde ones down below my boobs. I had them done in this place off Ken High Street up near where the original old Biba used to be. It took 3 hours for the man to do it, sticking them in with candle wax. and glue. God knows what my hair will look like when they come out and I am really pissed off because they are going to have to in about 2 weeks' time, as I've got to wear a wig in this play. It's an Oscar Wilde and there's no way I can stuff the dreads underneath. I tried with the help of the make-up lady, but I looked like I had a massive bush on my head – a burning bush at that as, in their wisdom, they've decided to make me a redhead which picks up nicely on every wretched freckle I've been trying to eliminate with lemon juice for the last ten years.

The other actors are very pleasant on the whole. Quite a bit older, apart from the bloke who plays the lead. The problem is, they are all doing the stock-in-trade Oscar Wilde performances and I want to explore the part and make it more interesting. I thought that's what rehearsals are for. You should be able to experiment in the first couple of weeks then, if it's not gelling, you drop it. However, the short-arse director can't see that and, of course, no one dares to say anything. Word gets around if you are a bit 'difficult'. It's the terror of never working again, especially if you are a woman. Men who voice their opinions are to be revered. I even heard of one famous actor considered in the biz as a 'dangerous beast,' which he must have loved. A woman expressing herself in the same way usually gets slung out unless she is famous. Even then, her reputation will proceed her like a bad smell.

There's only one famous person in this cast so the rest of us minnows have to keep shtum. Thinking about it, in this current climate, being a woman AND an actress probably leaves me just above an amoeba and somewhere below an illiterate male sex offender in terms of status. At least the only way is up.

"Youse not wanting more tea are youse?" the landlady dares me. Her Brummy accent is so weird. When I first arrived at the front door, I couldn't work out what she was on about. After a long while of me saying, "Sorry? What? I beg your pardon? Can you say that again?" she gave up and hauled me inside by my arm. Either she thought I was deaf or I was just a typical snotty Southerner pretending not to understand for the hell of it.

"No thanks," I reply. I don't think my internal organs can take any more ice-cold liquid. As it is, my throat probably resembles an Alpine slalom run. I need to get to the warmth of the rehearsal rooms before I seize up.

"Angela, don't you think it would be a good idea to move where you can hear your lead man?" The director drops his script to his side at the same time as his body does that sagging thing, just to emphasise the full extent of his exasperation. He's been like this ever since we started a week ago. The others look at their feet, aware that this is the third time he's had a go at me in the space of twenty minutes. Not that any of them bother to stand up for me. Bunch of wimps.

"Actually," I reply optimistically. "I thought Andy might have wanted to come to me as he's the one–"

"I don't care what you think and frankly, I am beginning to wonder if you think at all. Can you please get over to him and say your lines where he can see you." He does another of his exaggerated sighs, dropping his script as he slumps wearily at my stupidity and turns towards the company manager, rolling his eyes. I go and stand in front of the leading man and he gives me shifty eye contact because he's the biggest wimp of the lot. I'm wondering if I can bear the idea of being punished like this for another three and a half weeks. It's really messing with my head and I'm starting to think I can't act at all. I mean, even if I am a crap actor, it means nothing to me because I've always believed I am brilliant, ever since I gave the waiting world my Mole from Wind in the Willows at prep school. Once I heard the applause I knew that this was the life for me. I'd immersed myself in being a mole so completely that the world outside of 'Moley' was almost surreal because being a wild rodent was a whole lot more preferable than being a bewildered kid who no one seemed to want around. That's why I became an actress. It's really good fun because you get to be someone else who people seem to like - even a mole. Not to mention that this particular part I am doing was THE ONE that was going to put me on the map.

"Right Angela, move over there now – no, no, not there; there! For God's sake. Is it me? Am I speaking Urdu? Can you please listen to what I say–"

His voice trails off as I recognise that old familiar feeling of failing to get anything right. I've been here before. I've been here lots of times before when I was little…

"I can carry this for you, Mummy," I said, picking up a small Pyrex dish.

She seemed irritable and I thought she would be pleased to see us. "No Angela, you'll only drop it. I'll take it".

"No, Mummy," I wailed. "I want to take it. I won't drop it I promise." She really didn't understand how important this was. James and I hadn't seen her for weeks since she left us to live with Duncan, our stepfather, and we didn't know if she was ever coming back. I thought, if I got something right, she might want to come back and see us again. So here we were, helping her to move out of our lives.

"Oh alright, hurry up now," she sighed impatiently, picking up her box of belongings and setting off down the path. James and I trotted after her, down the cinder path, me with the Pyrex dish clutched tightly to my front, carefully choosing each step I took. But I needn't have bothered because, when I got there, the thing jumped out of my hands and broke into shards of glass at my feet. I couldn't believe it and I still to this day, didn't know how it happened.

"Oh, Angela!" barked my mother. "I knew you'd drop it." She picked up some of the larger bits and put them in her box of things and kicked the smaller bits into the undergrowth. Then, she left. We ran after the car for a short while and waved and waved until the car disappeared into the distance.

For weeks after, I could see glittering bits of glass amongst the crumbly black cinders. I'd crouch down and throw them into the long grass so I didn't have to be reminded of what happened. Then I would feel guilty because I thought the little field mice on their way home might cut their paws on it.

The thing is, if people think you are a failure, you become a failure, even if you aren't and right now, the director is doing what Mum did...

"Hello, Angela! Hello! Hello! Are you listening? If you like, the company can take a coffee break whilst you get yourself together? I mean obviously we aren't important compared to-" It isn't until I feel the sting of my dreadlocks slapping against my face that I understand what I'm doing. As I spin around to face him in my fury, they spin out like Medusa's snakes from my scalp and wallop me hard across my cheeks. The unexpected pain gives me such a shock that when I bellow at the little bugger, it sounds like a depth charge detonating. "WHY DON'T YOU FUCK OFF YOU BULLYING BASTARD. YOU FUCKING BULLY. FUCKING BASTARD. WHO THE FUCK DO YOU FUCKING THINK YOU ARE. BASTARD!"

Blimey, it's so loud, it even takes me by surprise, but there's no stopping me now and I'm running with it. I'm moving in on him, jabbing at his face with my finger. He tries to put up some kind of defence, but I've reached that point where I'm now gibbering with rage. "Don't think you can bully me, you little runt, because I've dealt with much worse from the king of fucking bullies - my bastard stepfather. You are nothing compared to him! You can stick your fucking job up your fucking arse. I don't need this shit." Then I stride out of the room, ignoring the rest of the company who are glued to the walls, like people on one of those fairground rides where the floor disappears and you're held up by the force of the spin.

I am so pissed off, I go and buy two Starbars and eat them all at once in the ladies and look at myself in the mirror. I look for signs of 'dumb insolence' in my expression or whatever it is that seems to set these people off. It strikes me that whatever you do, your past is always rising up to haunt you. It's like you can never get away from it. I thought leaving home, such as it was, meant that people would treat me differently. Everything that seems to happen to me triggers something in the past and I don't want the past.

The door to the ladies opens and the stage manager comes in and says the director wants to apologise to me, which he does; shows his soft underbelly like the snivelling cur he is.

Back in London again and I've moved out of my boyfriend's. No easy thing. He wasn't going down without a fight. He accused me of tangoing over his feelings in a pair of stilettos. It was pretty grim, especially when he got upset and kicked the electric fire which impaled itself on the end of his winklepicker so it shorted and the plug exploded. Then his mum answered the door when I went to pick up my last box of things and said that I was breaking his heart. What do you say to that? 'Oh. Ok. Well, I'll stay put then.'

I did feel sorry for him and I will miss being in the band which I really enjoyed. We had one more gig and then that was it.

Men are pragmatists. When they realise it's not going to work, they move on. I've seen it again and again. Eventually, even my dad had to throw in the towel over my Mum. He had to opt for what was realistic if he didn't want to die alone. Granted, my stepmother was a case of last chance saloon, but needs must.

Now, I rent a cupboard in a house with three other blokes. It's cheap. They call it the attic room but it's not, it's a cupboard. It looks like a cupboard from the outside and it's no bigger than a cupboard inside, except it hasn't any shelving. It opens directly onto some stairs. To your right, at the top of the stairs, there is just enough room for a single mattress on a ledge and the floor space extends a tiny bit behind the pillow so I can just squeeze my sound system in. You can't stand up in it unless the dormer window above the mattress is open (no good when it's raining or snowing, obviously), but you can climb out onto the roof if you fancy it. I keep my clothes in the so-called linen room, next to the bathroom. Mum would like this house. It's a middle-sized Georgian townhouse. Very nice.

Two of the other sharers are friends but were once lovers. Both Australian - but very different. One of them is a bit whiny and controlling. He keeps going up to the ponds at Hampstead and coming back with crabs - not for eating, you understand. He keeps the crab lotion in the bathroom cabinet but leaves it on the sink when he's having an attack, which I suppose is quite considerate. Without actually having to name the beast, he's letting us know we should take precautions, so I do. I scour the entire bathroom from head to toe before I use it - such a pain as it takes ages.

The other guy is a huge, jolly bear of a man. He's an anaesthetist and wears a big fur coat, which obviously I don't agree with. His excuse is that it's second-hand.

"It's not second-hand Gary," I said. "It's much more than second-hand and they are in fact paws not hands and there would have been a lot of them."

"Aw, Angela, don't make me feel guilty."

"Why not?"

"Because." He looks penitent to please me then puts it on and shuffles out the door. He parties nonstop and then goes off to hospital with a massive hangover and knocks people out. The third inhabitant works for the BBC Foreign Service and also reviews soul music for Time Out, so we have a good choice of sounds and parties most weekends with local bands from the pubs, including the one I'm in, rocking up after closing time. We all get on fine apart from the occasional spat with Crab Man.

I'm ok with the cupboard. I've lived in worse. When I was 12, the prefab we ended up in after running away from my stepfather was little more than a damp shack.

It's funny to think that if it wasn't for cats we would probably never have got away from him. It's worth noting that cats have played a very important part in my life and it began when Duncan had moved us up to Egham next to Windsor Park, roping his mother Jean in to stay with us. Jean had one of those horrid tight, purple perms on top of a face that was the shape of a cushion that had been sat on too many times; all puffed up and jowly round the edges. By the time she joined us, my stepfather no longer spoke to Mum or us kids, so it became her job to translate. Walking into the kitchen one day, forgetting to listen at the door to see if the coast was clear, I was confronted with mother and son reading their newspapers at the table. "Oh, sorry!" I started to back out.

"What do you want Angela?" asked Jean.

"Erm, can I get some milk please?"

Duncan looked back down at his paper. Jean turned to him. "Duncan, can Angela have some milk?"

A pause and then a sigh of irritation. "Yes."

"Yes, you may," replied Jean, like I was deaf or something. Blimey, I thought, they really are going round the twist, so I drank the milk as fast as I could, which resulted in hiccups. "You shouldn't gulp it down like that. Silly girl," said Jean.

Days later, she came downstairs, waving her nighttime potty at all of us. "Duncan! Duncan!" she called out. "Duncan, I want you to look at this." At first, I thought she'd gone gaga, after all, women of her age didn't normally go around showing people their number 2s did they? Even he looked worried. "Look what someone has done," she said, pushing it under his nose.

"Mother?" he said, flinching. "What are you doing? What's that?"

"Just take a look. It's disgusting. It's biggies!"

"Biggies? What do you mean?"

"Cat's biggies."

"Do you mean cat excrement? Can we leave the nursery behind and use the correct terminology? What's it doing in there?"

"That's what I want to know. Someone has obviously put it in there." With that, she went around showing the potty to us all with the 'biggies' in it. "What cat, I'd like to know, is clever enough to do its stuff in a potty?" she asked, looking pointedly at myself and James.

"Some cats are very intelligent," I mumbled. People really irritated me by the way they underestimated animals. "You're not telling me, Angela, a cat climbed into my potty to do its stuff. Next, you'll be telling me it used toilet paper to wipe itself!"

"But why would anyone want to do such a thing, Jean?" Mum asked. "I mean, what could they gain from it?"

"I don't know Helen, you tell me. It's quite revolting and whoever they are must have a very depraved sort of mind."

"What's so funny?" demanded my stepfather as James and I tried hard to stifle our giggles. "You think terrorising an old lady with animal excrement is amusing, do you?" We shook our heads. He turned on James. "I can see this would be the sort of thing you would find highly entertaining. This is your cat's stuff, isn't it?" 'Then, 'whoosh', he blew up, accusing James of all sorts of things and shouting at Mum, saying she had an Oedipus (that Greek bloke) complex and that he was sick and tired of us all. Honestly, I was at a loss to know how he could tell which cat's 'biggies' it was because we had two cats. Anyway, after he finally shut up and stormed off, James and I slunk upstairs. When Mum came up later, James hotly denied it all. Naturally, I took his side, although I'd never put anything past my brother. Next thing I knew, James was saying he was going to run away and I agreed to go with him. Dad's house was on the market and empty. He had moved up north so James reckoned we could at least stay there until we could find somewhere else. Mum didn't want to leave but I think she realised, at ages 12 and 14, she couldn't really stop us. After an hour or so of uhmming and aaahing, she finally agreed to come. The plan was she would call for a taxi the next morning when Duncan was taking his mother back to her horrible home in Bognor Regis. Then we'd all go down and stay in Dad's old house - the 'lovely house' as we called it, the one where we had spent two wonderful happy years away from Duncan. That is until Dad decided to disappear and we found ourselves back again with Mum and the tyrant. I never understood how, once you had been saved, you could be unsaved. I'd never read any books or seen any films where that happened.

That night, I packed all my stuff, half-excited and half-worrying Mum would pull out. The times we'd begged her to leave before and, to give her her due, she had scarpered a couple of times; once when she had just given birth to Boney at the nursing home - which wasn't great as she forgot to take us with her and left us with 'His Madness'. She ran off to hide at her sister's (my aunt Maddie). Unfortunately, Duncan found out, went round there and lobbed a brick through their window.

As you can imagine, Maddie and Uncle StJohn weren't best pleased, so Mum had to go back to him.

I tiptoed down to James's room to see what he thought. He looked steely, chewing his lip which he did when he was worried. He said he didn't care if Mum came or not, he was going anyway. I hardly slept a wink that night.

The taxi arrived the next morning and would you believe it, it was a bloody Mini! A tiny Mini to get me, James, Mum, Boney, our dog, Kiffa, two cats (Bully and Thenny) and all our cases in! Except it wasn't two cats because when we went to get Bully, he dodged out and ran away. He saw the cat basket and he was off. Mum said we would have to come back and get him and James and I were really upset because he was part of our family and we really didn't want to leave him behind. I said to Mum, "He'll think we're abandoning him." The taxi lady started getting impatient clucking and tutting so in the end we had to go. She wouldn't let our dog sit in the front, which we always let her do because in the back, she would bark the whole way, which is what she did in the woman's ear. Served her right for not taking our advice.

We lived at Dad's 'lovely house' for about three weeks. It wasn't easy because I knew we couldn't stay. The worst time was in the late afternoon when the sun became old and golden. The dying of the light always seems sad. I would go into Dad's bedroom and sit on the edge of his bed, looking out over the fields. The light made it feel like everything was slipping away. It made me think about everything I'd lost in my life so far; Dad and Bully - and the white kitten.

Ah yes, looking back, those were difficult times. And the white kitten. Well, I don't talk about that.

Chapter Five
SEX AIDS AND FAIRY DUST

1970's

I am now so broke, I'm having to hold down two jobs; one as a part-time outdoor clerk for a criminal lawyer and my other main one as a waitress in a wine bar. It's in Covent Garden and quite trendy. Obviously, the play up north - the one that was going to be 'THE ONE' - wasn't. It went well, but the director died from a stroke not long after I got mashed up on my motorbike travelling to the theatre in the last week of the run. He had to identify me because I was a bit of a mess and in and out of consciousness. Then he died 2 weeks later, which made me feel a bit guilty. Apparently, I had told him to go away. I only felt a bit guilty because he had a good life and a lovely wife and just about everything he wanted bar height, so he didn't do too badly and he shouldn't have been such a bully.

Since starting at the wine bar, quite a few people from my past have come in. One of the girls I worked with in the sex shop turned up. Bella is her name and she's now doing an M.A. in linguistics. I felt obliged to give her a free drink behind my boss's back and naturally, we got nattering about our time there. "Remember Billy, the manager? He and his colleagues were real gangsters from the East End and you know why he employed educated, posh girls like us, don't you? It gave the place a patina of respectability," Bella laughed. "I also think he quite liked the idea that I was gay."

"Yes," I agreed. "I think he thought it added a bit of spice."

My first day at the sex shop, I hoped I would fall down a sinkhole. I couldn't bring myself to look at the products, so I just stared at my feet and got pulled into the boss's office. I was very nervous of Billy the boss. Like all good East End gangsters, he lived at home with his mum but I knew intuitively that you never, ever wanted to cross him. If I'd told him to 'fuck off', I would have found myself hanging from a meat hook under a bridge somewhere in the East End..

As I stepped into his office, he looked me up and down and, pushing the heavy desk away with his feet, lolled back in his leather-winged armchair. His sharp-featured little girlfriend Nina perched, cross-legged, on an arm of the matching Chesterfield sofa. He had a cigar on the go and a tumbler of whisky which he swirled round and round like worry beads. His skin was the colour of uncooked suet, which looked even pastier against the backdrop of the dark red flock wallpaper and his pudding basin haircut, which I think was meant to look like the Beatles, was 10 years out of date, like his suit.

He flicked the end of his tie, eyeing me with a bemused expression. "Allo Ange."

"Hello," I squeaked.

"What's up then?" He put his head on one side.

What was up? What was he referring to? I didn't know. "Nothing," I replied nervously.

He smiled. "Yeah, that's what I thought. Nuffin." He turned to Nina and they exchanged a conspiratorial glance. "Listen Ange, luv, ain't Maureen told you what to do?"

"Er yes. Yes, she has."

"Yes, she has because she told me she has so... why ain't you fuckin' doin' it?" he asked nicely.

I thought it best just to look stupid and keep quiet. "See that?" he said pointing to a camera up on the wall. "That, my luv, shows me what you are up to ALL the time. Only place you are safe from it is in the ladies and, 'cos I'm a gentleman, I ain't gonna be puttin' it in there. See that?" He pointed again at an intercom on his desk. "That lets me talk to you lot. Now, the only time I want to do that is when one of you girls ain't doin her job - ain't walkin' round all the time, asking the punters what they want, sellin' them stuff. Do you get my drift?"

I got it. "See Ange, I ain't payin' for you to stand rooted to the spot lookin' at your tootsies for 8 hours a day now am I? 'Ain't gonna shift 300 newly arrived, state-of-the-art vibrators from Hong Kong with you doin' that now am I?"

"No," I said trying to laugh it off, at the same time thinking with horror, Vibrators!

"Good girl." He gave me a wink. It was like being blessed by the Pope.

Audience over, I bowed out of the door and went back on the shop floor. I bounded straight up to a pair of Latino-looking men sifting through a bin of multi-coloured clitoral stimulators - that's what it said on the box anyway. Most of them looked like they had the action of a cheese grater. Made me think of that old feminist joke: 'is it a plane? Is it a bird? No... it's a clitoris.' "Hello. Can I help you?" I said brightly, trying to sound normal.

The men looked up at me enquiringly. "Yes. Erm - we are from Argentina. Can you tell pleeease? Er - is theese the National Health Service?"

By the time 3 weeks had passed, I barely noticed the stock for what it was. I got really good at selling women's products that could be stuffed, winched or poked into almost every orifice imaginable, from duo balls (so-called) to French knickers (red or black pants with a whacking great dildo attached to the inside gusset). I did baulk at recommending one particular vibrator. It had a design on it like a totem pole with Tonto the Indian's face (he of the Lone Ranger) smiling on the tip. The cross-over from a character from childhood and sex was uncomfortable, but not as uncomfortable I thought as the thing itself once inserted. Its design feature allowed it to be cranked over at different angles so, if the user wasn't careful, it could have resulted in a painful D&C. 'Can we guess who designed that one?' I asked myself.

My biggest seller was the famous 'Stud Spray' which was basically a local anaesthetic for the old willy. The men all went for that in the insane belief that women wanted to be pulverised by an unfeeling nob for hours on end. Honestly, so many men seemed to think sex was all about drilling holes and taking a short time about it. I thought they confused it with D.I.Y. I overheard one man, a lawyer type, complaining about the spray to his friend as they perused our latest offers. "For God's sake, don't touch that whatever you do," he warned, sifting through some edible knickers as his friend scanned the claims on the packaging with hope.

"Really?"

"Really," he affirmed. "I used it on the wife and what I thought were cries of pleasure turned out to be groans of pain. It numbs the old chap. Can't feel a thing so you're batting away with no sensation and you both end up red raw. Damn thing stayed hard for hours. Still standing to attention saluting on the tube to work the next day. Ghastly!"

By the fourth week, I pulled off my first bonus. The only products worth bonuses hung out in the 'Rubber' cabinet which lurked in a dimly lit corner away from the main thoroughfare. At first, I dreaded being corralled over there and used to accelerate past it, but there was money to be made, so I put on this matter–of–fact–nanny–knows-best sort of voice, and pretended to myself I was selling nothing more interesting than grommets.

The inane-looking 'Blow–up Helga Doll', which at least had a face, could earn you an extra fiver, but the female torso (no arms, no legs, no head) made out of durable rubber (supposedly due to the hammering it was going to get) could pull you in a glorious tenner. The double dildo and the vibrating vagina were worth seven quid each. The latter, a grizzly piece by anyone's standards, better suited to the chamber of horrors, was so revolting, I could hardly bear to look at it. At first, I thought it was a squashed hedgehog, but on closer inspection, it reminded me of a large Ginster's Cornish pasty with fake, wiry, pubic hair and a vibrator stuck up one end. Honestly, you have to ask yourself what had any of this got to do with actual women? It was like parts of their anatomy chopped up and sold like pieces of meat at a butcher's. I had to put all those feelings of disgust aside because, finally, I was earning a decent wage and could help Mum a bit and, in the end, it wasn't going to be my life's work. I'd just have to pick up the baton for women's rights later on in my life.

"Got a nice creep there by the looks," said Maureen, the deputy boss, drawing on her 50th fag as she handed me the key to the rubber cabinet. "Think I seen 'im before. Try and push the torso luv, get yerself a tenner." I got myself a fiver in the end with the sale of my first Helga Doll to the man in black-rimmed glasses who never once looked me in the eye.

I stayed at the sex shop until the so-called 'winter of discontent' when something happened which sounded the death knell for my time there.

"Hello Billy, it's Angela. I just wondered if we are coming into work tonight as there's no lighting?" I'd rung in expecting/hoping to be laid off.

"Of course you are. I ain't losing business cos that pratt Ted friggin' Heath and his nancy boys are lettin' them fuckin' Unions ride roughshod over 'em. What is he, a man or a mouse? Bloody ridiculous!"

"Ah."

"I want you to work up the Shaftesbury Avenue store, but come into the main shop first and Maureen will give you a couple of paraffin lamps. Alright?"

"Er yes," I replied, considering the upside and the downside of the arrangement. "Will I be on my own?"

"To start with luv, but I'll send Little John up later."

Little John was Billy's small, fat gofer. He was alright in a dense, pie-eating, sort of way. I wasn't sure I wanted to be on my own with only the light of two smelly paraffin lamps. Since there was no electricity, I couldn't even play some music, so for a fleeting moment, even the reduced company of Little John had its attractions when I considered the long, freezing-cold evening ahead of me. I couldn't imagine there would be many people about wanting to peer at sex aids. Again, it was money and I had now bought myself a second-hand Austin 1100 which I'd got because I couldn't stand biking it in the winter.

Driving through the dark streets of London, I turned into Piccadilly and parked up. No need to worry about double yellows tonight. I grabbed the keys to the shop, picked up the paraffin lamps, then whizzed up to Shaftesbury Avenue. Hardly anywhere was open and there was no one about. A damp November fog has settled upon the city, adding to the gloom.

Inside, I tidied the magazines and blocked off the stairs to the basement where the film booths were. I hunkered down on the stool behind the counter, counting the minutes and hoping I would be allowed to close early. A stray couple emerged out of the mists looking in for a quick giggle and the owner of the Chinese, which was shut next door, popped his head round to say 'hi', which was friendly, but otherwise nothing and nobody.

I'd just read another load of 'housewives 'true' porn experiences, when in walked a tall, well-dressed man wearing an expensive Burberry Mac and a sharp-looking hat. I smiled at him and said 'hello' to which he grunted something in reply. He walked over to the magazines displayed across the back wall and started flicking through them. I was just thinking what a coup it would be if I managed to sell something, when suddenly, out of nowhere, a howl of anger split the silence and the man turned round yelling at the top of his voice. "You filthy whore! You dirty bitch! Stinking prostitute!" He started shredding the magazine he held in his hands, tearing through a block of pages with maniacal strength before flinging what was left to the ground. Next thing I knew, he'd swung round, sweeping all the magazines off the shelf, ranting about whores and filth and started on the products. I jumped off my stool and crouched down behind the counter, watching in alarm as dildos and clitoral stimulators whistled through the air. Coloured condoms were torn from their packets and flung on the floor and a pair of duo balls were launched at the counter like Mexican Bolas. When there was nothing left to throw, he fell upon the centre stand, roaring like a maddened gorilla, determined to wrench it up, despite it being solidly nailed to the floor. It was pretty worrying. I was stuck with no escape route because every which way was blocked by him. It then occurred to me he might just finish off his mad session by whipping his todger out and doing something foul because sex loonies do that sort of thing you know, and then, as my mind raced on in panic, I thought, maybe he doesn't have a todger and that's what all the fuss is about, or maybe it's weenie and someone's commented on it – probably a woman - ah, that's it - maybe I should direct him to the strap on penis extension, obviously when he'd calmed down a bit, because given his frame of mind, producing a large, fake cock at this juncture, probably wouldn't help the situation.

Just as suddenly as he started, he stopped. In the silence, I could hear him panting. He looked around at his handiwork, then his gaze settled on me. I mean fixed on me. There was a large marble ashtray just up on the counter to my right. He slowly walked towards me, crunching sex aids underfoot. As he approached, he slipped his hand into his breast pocket like one of those gangsters. 'Oh no! He's got a gun. He's going to kill me. I've hardly lived and I'm going to die in a sex shop. Mum will never live it down. No!' My hand shot out to grab the ashtray. I raised it up high to give it as much velocity as I could when I brought it down upon him, hoping he didn't shoot me first. His hand stopped moving as we stared at each other. Then he slowly brought it out. No gun. Phew! He remained motionless, eyeballing me with a sneer twitching the side of his mouth then turning suddenly, with a final parting, 'fucking whore', he left the shop and disappeared into the darkness of the Conservative government's streets. I stayed behind the counter, my fingers clamped around the ashtray just in case he came back. The shop was a mess, but I wasn't taking the risk of leaving my safe place. It made me feel all jangly.

What was strange was the sense of Déjà vu. I'd certainly never met that man before, but it was the expression on his face. I knew that look from somewhere else. Of course. Duncan.

Duncan and the chocolate cake.

I was eight at the time and it was the first time I surprised myself with a reaction that came out of nowhere. I was licking out a cake bowl, chatting to Mum, when the door opened and Duncan walked in. I did my usual thing of trying to shrink. I believed, if I was smaller, he wouldn't notice me, which was a bit stupid. "Go and wash that up," he commanded. I looked over to Mum for backup.

"I said she could," she murmured.

"Go and wash it up," he repeated, ignoring her. I looked back at her but she'd had her stab at it so she just dropped her head. I understood why, but I still felt a bit let down.

"Mummy said I could lick it," I muttered.

"Don't argue with me. Do as you're told!" I realised he was beginning to get agitated. He had that look in his eyes which meant that at any minute, he would explode.

I was going to give in when, out of nowhere, I heard myself saying, "You can't tell me what to do. Only my daddy can tell me what to do. You are a bloody man.

You're a bloody man!" and then I threw the bowl down and ran. I ran for what I thought was my life.

I could hear him shouting, "Angela! Angela! Come back here!" but I wasn't stopping. I dodged up the back stairs and hammered down the landing to my room. No one ever defied him and got away with it, least of all a scrawny 8-year-old, and I absolutely believed he would come after me and kill me; on top of which, he would probably torture me first for using the word 'bloody'. When I reached my room, I realised I had a major problem because it was the dressing room to the large bedroom next door where my little brother, Boney, had his cot. It had a door to that and another main one onto the front stairs. That meant I had to keep two separate doors shut against the killer and neither had a lock. That really panicked me. I ran from one to another like a headless chicken, not knowing what to do. Then I decided he'd most likely go for the main door first, so I thought I'd hold onto the doorknob to that one and put a chair up against the other. I looked down at my weedy little wrists and willed them to have the strength to keep him out. I held on and I waited. He didn't come immediately. Mum must have managed to delay him but, as I was gabbling away to God - "Please God, help me! Please God, help me," - I heard his footsteps pounding down the landing. I started sweating and my hands went all slippy on the doorknob and I had to keep wiping them down my front. He came to a stop outside my room and then, after what seemed an age, said in a very calm, slimy voice, which made it even more horrid, "Angela?"

No reply.

"Angela?"

Silence.

And then he tried the doorknob.

I held onto it with all my strength so my knuckles went white and I said to myself over and over, "You will not get me. You will not get me. You will not get me." I didn't think I could hold onto it much longer when, all of a sudden, he stopped. For a moment, I thought he'd given up but then realised, with a sickening lurch, he was creeping round to try the other door. I ran to it just in time as he pushed it open a crack, but the chair held and I slammed against it with my body. "Angela," he said in a wheedly sort of voice like he was this gentle, reasonable person. "Angela, I need to talk to you." I mean, whatever made him think I would fall for that one? I'd crossed the line and there was no way back, except death. I shot back to guard the other door as I heard him move off again and then it all went quiet, apart from the sound of my heart which seemed like it was going to burst out of my ears. Nothing happened for what seemed like ages and then I heard his footfall going down the stairs. I stayed by the door in case he doubled back. After a while, my heart calmed down a bit and I started to breathe properly again. I looked around my room. It was pretty small with just my bed and drawers and bedside table in it and I wondered what I was going to do. If I was going to keep him at bay, it would mean I could never sleep again, never eat again, never see our dog and cats again and where was I going to go to the lavatory? I know it sounds stupid but I was only eight and, like I said, I was really frightened. In some ways, it was quite good for me because nobody really frightens me now.

Eventually, Mum came up. I reckon something must have been said about my dad because my dad was still in love with my mum and, when I think about it, I expect my stepfather was frightened I would tell my father and he'd come over and give him a bloody nose. But children don't tell and, in any case, you just think it's your life. When Mum finally convinced me that he wasn't going to flay me alive and pin my carcass to the front door, I went downstairs. I gave it 3 hours before I did though, just to make sure he'd simmered down. Fortunately, he avoided me as much as I avoided him. Nevertheless, I made sure the chair was left up against the other door in case he had a change of heart in the night.

My stepfather's middle name was Rudolph. You'd think someone called Rudolph would be a nice person, wouldn't you? Santa Claus's best reindeer and all that. But the truth was, it was like calling Hitler 'Flopsy Bunny' or Stalin 'Cuddles'. Duncan was our very own dictator.

"What the fuck's gone on 'ere?" exclaimed Little John appearing suddenly out of the gloom, making me jump.

"This man came in and went mad," I said.

"Did 'ee? Well, Billy's gonna go friggin' mad with all his stock being mashed up like that. Get over there and get them magazines and then 'elp me put the other stuff away." He shook his head. "Ain't no good leavin' a fuckin' woman on her own to 'andle things."

I found out how he handled things one spring evening 3 months later, in another of their satellite shops. I was doing the rounds, trying to sell stuff to the punters, when a man came in and paid to go downstairs to see a film in one of the cubicles. I didn't think anything of it but Little John followed him down. Bolting back up, red in the face, he grabbed a pair of scissors from the side of the till and hissed through gritted teeth, "Fuckin' bastard's stealing the film ain't he?"

"Oh. Shall I call the police?"

"Nah, nah," he answered, his eyes fixed on the stairs. "Stay there and don't move. I'm gonna sort the bastard out."

And he did. The man came bounding up the stairs and ran full tilt into the scissors as Little John leapt forward and thrust them into his stomach. The man stopped, looked surprised, dropped the film out from under his jacket and ran off into the crowds. There was blood on the scissors and blood on the floor. It was horrible. It was horrible and unnecessary. That was it for me. I'd more or less decided by then I'd had enough, but that was the catalyst and I handed in my notice with a request that Billy arranged to blow up my car as it wasn't going very well after some idiot had stolen it and dumped it in a field in Hertfordshire. It was Billy's parting bonus for me, which was nice of him, but boy was I glad to leave that world behind. Sex had become a complete turn-off after having it stuffed down my throat (so to speak) 7 days a week. I didn't want to hear about it, read about it, talk about it, see it, do it – NOTHING! I was totally turned off. It all seemed so silly. People got so worked up about sex - busy trying to find things to make it more exciting than it actually is. My friend Jen went out with a man who she regularly had to strip naked, blindfold, tie to a chair, leave in a room for 10 minutes to ferment, then go back in and whip him like a dog! Apparently, he liked the sound of the whip whistling through the air before it walloped him. I don't know why he didn't just join the army.

Seeing Bella in the wine bar again and hearing how her life was motoring forward - studying for an M.A. and buying a flat with her girlfriend - made me realise that I had more or less achieved nothing. I managed to pay Mum's big bills for a time but that was some while back and the plan to become the next major superstar wasn't making headway. "You should buy a flat, Angela," Bella said as she sipped her third free glass of wine.

"With what?" I asked, thinking what doesn't she get? "Bella, I'm a flipping waitress earning bugger all. My acting career right now is non-existent so I can barely afford to rent the cupboard I sleep in. Where does buying a flat feature in that?"

"Oh, it's easy. You don't need any money." She looked smug - not a good look when you are sporting a mullet left over from Bay City Roller days of non-fashion.

"Really? How does that work?"

"You just tell them you are doing a high-powered, self-employed job and give them an official bit of paper with your grossly over-estimated wages on, find the right lawyer and Bob's your uncle."

"Really? It's as simple as that?"

"Yup," she replied, lighting up another fag.

For a moment, time froze. To have my own home. Was that possible? "You're kidding." I looked at her in disbelief.

"No, I'm not. That's how I've done it. It's Maggie Thatcher's self-certification wheeze. You probably need to find someone who runs their own business to make it look official on their headed paper, then once you've got that, it's full steam ahead."

A home of my own! It was as if Tinkerbell had zapped me with her wand. My mind started whirring. I could get a house and let out a room to pay the mortgage and then I might be able to wangle a house for my mum if it was that easy. Wow! My heart started to pound with excitement. That meant I could afford to fail. I no longer had to be grotesquely successful because I could achieve what I wanted with lies and bits of paper. I could almost feel the fairy dust falling on my head. "I'll give you the telephone number of the lawyer I used if you like. He doesn't ask questions." Bella gave a wink.

"Fantastic," I replied, topping up her glass. "That would be absolutely fantastic. Thanks, Bella." I grabbed a pen. "And his name is?"

"Bender. Mr Robert Bender of Camden Town."

Chapter Six
RUN RABBIT RUN

1980's

I found the solicitor's offices in a run-down old building off Holloway Road, his name written on a bit of old paper squeezed behind well-fingered plastic coating. "Let's hope Bender is as Bender does," I said to myself as I bounded up the dark staircase with its scuffed wallpaper and bare light bulb adding to the general neglect. In my bag, I carried the important document I had somehow wangled my friend, Mo, to get her boss, Jack, to do for me. I'm not sure why he did it, just kind I suppose. Nice looking too.

I was feeling a bit nervous in case the lawyer started asking me questions about what film producing entailed, as I actually had no real idea beyond the fact that I knew they raised money and sort of collated everything together. I'd toyed with wearing a really short Ra-Ra skirt to help things along, even though it cut right across my feminist principles, but this was too important to be shackled by principles. I decided against it in the end, reasoning if I was parading as a producer, it would be better to dress more conservatively, knowing that men find it difficult to equate female intelligence with overt female sexiness. I shouldn't have worried. Bob Bender was not in the least bit interested in the people who beat a path to his door, attractive or otherwise. As long as you had the money, he did the work and seemed to be quite content scratching out a living. There was just one glitch. I had seen a flat which would have been ideal. There was a small problem with the central heating since the boiler was housed in the garden shed and so the pipes had to travel through the garden before coming in through the wall of the kitchen. Other than that, it seemed ideal. It was quite big and not too far from the tube, but it turned out the price was a bit too high for my fake earnings. "I'm afraid, unless you can get them to come down or your wages up, you won't get the 100% mortgage you need. Unless your seller is going to drop the price." Bender looked at me disinterestedly as he handed me back my precious document.

"Oh. How much more do I need?" I asked, knowing the seller wouldn't budge. She was a crazy South African woman who lived with her grown-up son. I think funds had run out and neither appeared to work.

"Well, I should say to be on the safe side another £4,000." 4 thousand! How was I going to raise that?

"I see," I replied, trying to look cool. "Well, I am... erm... due a raise." I knew it was a transparent lie, but I didn't care. Bender didn't either. He'd probably heard more unlikely tales than mine. "So, I suppose the best thing for me to do would be to go back to the company and have a chat."

"Yes. You do that," he said, lighting another cigarette from the existing one burning in the ashtray. The walls were rag-rolled in nicotine. "Goodbye." He reached for the telephone, signalling our meeting was at an end. I liked Bender's peremptory manner. It suited both of us to spend as little time as was necessary in one another's company and, in any case, I had to get over to Knightsbridge Crown Court. I had a hearing there representing the solicitor as an outdoor clerk (ME representing a solicitor! No wonder the legal system is a joke) and I was running late. By the way, the irony of my situation hadn't escaped me.I had been a minor thief myself from the age of 4 and a half , under the tutelage of my older brother James. Old 'light fingers' herself representing law and justice. I still dabbled on the odd occasion, but I'd been put off a while back when a boyfriend of mine got done for nicking (at my insistence) some jeans from the warehouse he worked at. I know poverty was no excuse, but we both worked full time and only had enough money to pay the rent on a shared house near Golders Green and I so wanted some nice trendy jeans.

It was 2 in the morning when we were woken from our slumbers by the cops banging on the door. "Hey, come on guys," joked my cocky Australian boyfriend. "Don't you think it's a bit early in the morning to be playing Starsky and Hutch," that was before he got flattened behind the door as they stampeded through. Hearing the commotion, I leapt out of bed, naked, and scrabbled to find his passport, knowing his visa had run out. I flung it out of the back window into the garden and it sailed into the hands of a waiting copper who got a good eyeful at the same time.

We were hauled off to Paddington Station where all the IRA suspects went and put in separate rooms where we were interviewed.The big beer-gutted, pock-marked Glaswegian stared at me across the table. "You're a nice enough birrrrrd. I wud cut 'n rrrrun if I was yoose. Find someone betterrr," he said with a leer.

"I hope you're not applying for the post," I replied. His leer reduced to a sneer.

When I went on to say that I thought allocating 3 policemen for 2 pairs of jeans of which they had no proof were stolen in the first place seemed a bit OTT, considering the ever-growing threat of being bombed by the IRA, he got more than a bit spiky. Once he'd quietened down, he growled. "The drugs we found in this house-"

"Not ours," I interrupted. "They belonged to our housemates that are away for the weekend, I told you."

"Aye but," he snarled." Where's your evidence?"

"They were in the drawer in his room, not ours."

"Means nothing. Whose to say you dinney share them or just keep them stashed there?"

"We don't use drugs."

"Aye wee girly, but whose to believe you? You were the one throwing the passport oot the windy. Does nae look verra innocent to me does it noo? Look, I'm nae interested in the visa or the drugs. I came to get your man done for the jeans. That's it."

In the end, he did a deal and my boyfriend got his visa sorted, but he had to go to court for the stolen jeans and unfortunately, on the day of his hearing, he was booked in to get the hoover fixed which was long overdue. I forced him to do it because the house was covered in dog hair since my mum had left her darling dog with us (she was once again homeless). He took it with him to get mended afterwards. When his case came up, he couldn't get anyone at the court to look after it, probably because at that time, everybody thought everything was a bomb and a vacuum cleaner-sized bomb would clear the entire building, so he was forced to go into the witness box with it. The Beak asked him why he had it - if it was a co-defendant and whether it bore any relevance to his case. This apparently made everyone in the courtroom snigger. For some reason, he found this deeply humiliating, more so than being dragged off to a police station in the middle of the night and getting a criminal record. He blamed me for making him take the thing. That was the end really of our relationship. He obviously lacked a sense of humour. In any case, the hoover was unfixable and he had to buy a new one and, on the plus side, the woman who sold it to him he later married so I don't know what he was whining about.

Anyway back to the day in hand, I'd managed to swap my day shift for the evening one at the wine bar, so today was going to be a long one.

Lawyers are funny people. This one I worked for part-time was pretty weird. A small, podgy, balding Jewish guy obsessed with sex and constantly at war with his mother. On one occasion, she had starfished herself on the drive, trying to prevent him from leaving whilst in the middle of one of their legendary rows. He took affirmative action and ran her over in his car, that's what he said. He said he just gently rolled over her neck.

"You can't just gently roll over someone's neck in a car and expect them to live," I expostulated.

"She's Jewish for Chrisssake!" he replied wearily, like I was some kind of a moron and should know that Jewish women have necks made out of rock from the earth's core. He stuck to his story tenaciously, just as his clients did to their misdemeanours, who were all as guilty as hell and made up mostly of feckless drug addicts and small/medium-time criminals.

He left me in charge of the office one summer's day so he could take his small workforce out for a long lunch. I sat at his desk, ready to man the phones with instructions that he was busy at court and would respond as soon as he returned. Time dragged by. After I had tried unsuccessfully to use my time to work out my next master plan, read two more chapters of my book and daydreamed for a good 40 minutes, I was restless. I decided to have a poke around. In the corner of the room was a large filing cabinet which looked innocuous enough. To my surprise, it wasn't locked which, considering the sensitivity of what it held, was pretty lax. It was all the criminal files ongoing and recent. I flicked through idly until I saw one that had photos attached. It was the case of a Geoffrey Pace of London EC1. Ignoring the blurb, I went straight for the photos. At first, I couldn't work out what I was looking at then, as I turned them this way and that, it gradually dawned on me I was looking at the image of a man's head that had been pulverised. The face no longer resembled a face. There was an eye hanging off a cheekbone and the rest was mostly blood and gore! Murder! I was looking at someone who had been brutally murdered! Flustered, I pushed the file back into the drawer and slammed it shut. I sat at the desk, eying the cabinet. This was a far cry from the pitiful people I was sent to court to oversee, who filed in through the office's open door in Bayswater. On the whole, the clients were an inoffensive bunch, and in the case of young Mr Jericho, who I was representing later on that day, and whom I had actually met before at another court hearing only a few weeks earlier, actually very pleasant.

As I ran up the steps of Knightsbridge, Mr Jericho was standing at the top drawing on a fag, chatting to a good-looking, public school boy type in his early twenties. We excused ourselves and moved away. "Oh no, Mr Jericho, you're here again," I said, giving him that half-sorry, half-smiling, half-tsk-tsk-tsk-what-are-we-going-to-do approach with a touch of 'you're in 'Nanny's safe hands' thrown in. This was the role I plumped for when being an outdoor clerk so that they didn't realise I was a complete fraud and so far, it seemed to work.

Mr Jericho smiled broadly and nodded. "I know." He then made that sucking noise Jamaican folk make through their teeth.

"What is it this time?" I asked.

"Receiving stolen goods," he replied, his smile getting wider.

"Oh, Mr. Jericho, why did you do that - I mean, how come they are prosecuting you for that?" I quickly corrected myself; 'Must remember not guilty until blah blah.'

"I was just lookin' after some stuff for my friend. I didn't know it was stolen." He shook his head.

"Ah," I replied. "Not sure the judge is going to be too pleased. Second time in 3 weeks for another offence." Mr Jericho looked at me still smiling. In spite of his jolly countenance, I could tell that wasn't what he wanted to hear. "See what our barrister says anyway," I added, trying to sound positive but I knew, just as he did, this was a no goer and it was more than likely that the barrister was going to suggest a guilty plea to the judge so that the sentencing wouldn't be so harsh for wasting court time. In Mr Jericho's case, I knew he would see sense but convincing our other more hopeless clients wasn't so easy – like poor Mr Andrews. The barrister had a way of telling people like Mr Andrews what the score was in a very British, palatable way.

"Now, Mr Andrew," the silver-tongued barrister began, flicking a glance over to me as he talked down at the feckless druggy. "The problem we have here is this; when you were found in your flat with 3 kilos of heroin, scales, plastic bags, several packs of needles and a wadge of money amounting to £785 in the telephone directory secreted behind the bookcase, it didn't look like it was merely for your own consumption. Naturally, I, as your brief and Miss Fleming here, your solicitor's representative, believe you, but we have to ask ourselves, will the court? The problem being, we have no evidence or witnesses to the contrary." Most of the wretches capitulated like the sensible Mr Jericho and went for a deal, but every now and then, you got one like Mr Andrews who was prepared to take the gamble. As they did on their lives. Neither of which paid off. I didn't like doing stuff with the addicts. They were so pathetic in the real sense of the word and gave me a worrying sense of foreboding about where James was heading.

There is something so degrading about being in the pay of a drug. I mean it's bad enough when you allow another human being to control you, but a frigging drug? It was a real shame about Mr Jericho because he was such a pleasant man - unruffled, easygoing, laughed at my jokes. He was bound to meet all kinds of unsavoury types in prison and I got the feeling he was someone who could easily be persuaded.

"By the way," I asked Mr Jericho, as we turned to go into the court building. "That young guy you were talking to. What was he up for?"

"Rape," he replied, his smile vanishing as he looked into the middle distance.

"Rape?" I echoed in disbelief.

He nodded. "Second time."

"My God! Why wasn't he put away the first time?"

"I don't know," he replied, looking at the ground. "I didn't like to ask. Wasn't quite right, if you know what I mean."

"Bastard should be flogged," I said vehemently. Mr Jericho looked disconcerted at the change in Nanny.

I feel knackered. I got back last night after working for the solicitor and doing a late shift. I feel a bit despondent about young Mr Jericho (who sad to say received a prison sentence due to his recidivism), only to find that James had been round and left again with my sound system. Plus he'd borrowed my flatmate's car without asking. He'd returned the latter but there's no sign of my stuff. I've now got to go and confront him which I don't want to do because I hate confrontation and I just know he's going to lie. It's his stock-in-trade. I think he actually prefers lying to telling the truth. Bloody hell.

All the curtains are drawn. I've rung the bell but no one's answering. I know he's in there. His beautiful cat appears at my feet and arches her back in welcome, reaching up with her perfect little nose. "Hello, sweetie." I bend down to stroke her. She has very soft, long fur and very large, sad eyes which reminded me of the paintings I used to see in our local Co-op furniture store of abnormal-headed children with huge tears sliding down their cheeks. I press the doorbell again and shout. "James! James, are you in there?" I hear a door bang within and finally, James appears. He doesn't look good.

"Hello, Ange. Sorry, I was in the bog." His eyes are red and the pupils pinpricks. "Come in, come in," he says, trying to avoid eye contact and turning back into the house.

"No, I don't want to come in. I want to know where my sound system has gone to?"

"Your sound system?" His speech is slurred.

Here we go. "Yes, James my sound system. You were seen loading it into my flatmate's car, who, by the way, was not happy about you borrowing it. Without permission."

"Yes, alright, alright. Keep your hair on." Already he's put me on the defensive like I'm an unreasonable hysteric overreacting. "Look, come in will you? I don't want to discuss this in the doorway."

I stand my ground. "There's nothing to discuss. I want it back. Where is it?"

"Look for fuck's sake, just get in I don't want the old woman next door listening. Trouble enough from her as it is." He shuffles off muttering and I, as usual, am forced to follow. The door to the marijuana plant room is ajar and I catch sight of upturned tubs and old newspapers scattered across the floor. No sign of the serried ranks of the much-pampered cannabis and a cold draft emanates from the room. With a lurch of fear, I realise, if they are off the menu, then things have taken a nosedive.

Inside the sitting room, there's a mess of old coffee mugs, baccy and rizlas. Cigarette burns scar the edge of the table even his precious Bible - Castenadas' 'Teachings of Don Juan' - has had bits of the cover torn off for a roach. There's a bloke asleep in one of the chairs, except he's not really asleep. "Hey man, wake up, this is my sister," orders James as if getting a visit from an important dignitary. He's making an effort to show me respect because he is going to have to try and keep me calm over my stolen goods. But I'm not calm and I'm not going to be taken in by any of his stories. The bloke struggles to stir himself and manages to open his eyes for a second, gives an inane grin then his eyeballs swivel up into his skull and he slumps back into the chair.

My sound system has gone into their veins.

I look at James struggling to roll himself a cigarette and I realise with a sudden internal burst of emotion that I'm looking at the wreckage of my brother. What he has become and what he could have been is now slipping away and he's not fighting to hold on to it. "James," I blurt out. "What are you doing?"

"Uhmm?" he replies, concentrating on licking along the seam of the roll-up.

"What are you doing?"

"Now, look here man," he says, adopting the transatlantic, hippy style talk that seems to grab him whenever under the influence of anything narcotic. "I will get your stuff back. I just lent it to someone because they were having this big do and y'know... I owed the dude a favour. He's been a good mate, y'know... and there was no money right..."

"No," I interrupt. "WHAT are you doing?" Pause. I can't name it. I don't want to give it its name because if I do, we can't pretend anymore. I struggle to sound cold and detached but I can feel my voice catching. "You will lose everything. It won't come back to you. Please. Please stop." James doesn't answer. The man in the chair belches loudly, then shifts his position.

"Oi! Have some respect!" James admonishes. The bloke grunts.

James shrugs. "As far as I'm concerned, the world is a pile of shit, always has been, so what's to lose?" I feel myself sinking in the face of his nihilism.

"But... well, what about us? Me and Mum and-?"

He snorts. "What about you?"

"We care about you. We want you to be happy."

"Happy?" he interrupts angrily. "Grow up Angela, why don't you? There's no such fucking thing. What do we know about happiness? Stuff like that just pisses me off. Look, best thing you can do is leave me alone. You're really hassling me."

I'm not sure he gets the wrongness of what he's just accused me of, but I can't bring up the business of my sound system again because I know we have moved into a much darker place.

"But surely..." I begin, but he cuts across me.

"Listen," he drawls. "If it makes it any easier for you, understand this; I don't care about you, so you don't have to care about me." Then he gives a horrid, wry little laugh and settles back in the chair, watching me with a cold smile.

So, I leave.

I walk down the road and keep walking. Sometimes I run. I walk and run until I reach Primrose Hill and, at the top, I sit down on the grass and think about Mr and Mrs Pongo of 'One Hundred and One Dalmatians'. How they came here to do their twilight barking. I got that book for Christmas one year at the old house we lived in with Duncan. I know James hates Christmas, but I really like it despite the bad ones we had with Duncan, who seemed to see it as an occasion to indulge his own particular brand of Gestalt therapy. At the drop of a scalding potato, he would bellow, slam doors, fling pudding and stamp on presents. The stains on the ceiling where the cranberry sauce got splattered during one of his more spectacular explosions, remained there until we moved out.

Christmas... Ah yes, there I was, padding quietly along the cold, dark landing of the old house to my brother's bedroom, carrying my bulky stocking. James was already rummaging through his. I jumped on his bed and we slung the mandatory tangerines and nuts to one side and compared with squeaks and squeals the presents Mum had pushed into old woollen socks. "Let's go down and see the tree," I whispered. We crept down the creaky wooden back stairs, through the kitchen, across the flag-stoned passageway into the hall, then opening the door into the drawing room, we were confronted with the most wonderful Christmas scene. Handmade golden angels trumpeted their jubilation around the central light, intricate snowflakes made out of silver paper trailed from the ceiling and, behind it all, standing in the alcove, in green-skirted splendour, a 7-foot Christmas tree adorned with gleaming baubles and yew-berry-red candles. We giggled and gasped with delight. You had to hand it to Duncan, the old tyrant, he was very creative. We fell upon the presents around the tree to see who had the biggest and were busy feeling and shaking them, guessing what they might be when.

"What do you think you are doing?"

We whipped round to see the apoplectic figure of Duncan. He stepped towards us and wrenched the parcel out of James' hands. "Why is it you have to ruin everything for everyone? Go back to your beds at once and don't make another sound until you are called. Other people want to enjoy Christmas – it's not all about you." We shuffled past him, back to our freezing-cold rooms, knowing that, if he started off badly, he only ever got worse, so the day became much like any other, where we kept out of the way, cowed but inwardly defiant.

I lie back on the cold grass. I don't understand why James has given up. He is forgetting we were brothers in arms. We are each other's witness. He's my pack. How can he cut us loose? It's like I'm running a race and, when I look back, I can see James has fallen but, when I run back to pick him up to save him, he pushes me away. He has a new friend now. One that is dragging him back by his ankles to the starting line. Perhaps that's the best place to be; always at the starting line. Don't take part. Never try, just give up.

I stare into the dark and search for stars. Sometimes, you can catch sight of Venus, the first star of the evening, in spite of the sodium glow, but often, what you think is a star is a piece of human junk or an aeroplane toiling their way through the heavens. "Hello Angela, what are you doing?" I freeze. The dark figure of a man is standing over me silhouetted against the skyline. I scramble to get up. "No. No. Don't stir yourself on my account," he says. As he does, I feel his hand on my shoulder.

"Sorry, who are you?" I ask, trying to sound in control, because there is something familiar about the voice, like a bad feeling.

The voice gives a hollow laugh. "Don't you know?"

Fear rushes through my body.

"I wondered how…" he begins, but I don't hear the rest. I'm gone - running as fast as I can down the hill.

'Oh Christ, Oh Jesus bloody Christ, what is going on? Run, run, run, faster, keep going, don't look behind, don't stop, keep going, run, run, for god's sake how can… how can it be? Lungs burning, run, run. It can't be, it can't be… can it? CAN IT?' Slamming in through the doors of a pub, the startled punters turn and look at me accusingly, jolted out of their pleasure bubbles. I'm pumping like a steam train, hair stuck to my forehead with sweat. "Training for the marathon are you luv?" asks one.

"Yeah. That's right," I puff. "Need the loo." I head for the ladies, ignoring the barman muttering about treating his pub as a public convenience. I lock the door and stand on the loo seat just in case. Just in case.

Chapter Seven
LAUGHTER AND THE MOON

"Hello, Jack," I say in a suitably apologetic, cringing voice. I am back in the offices of my friend Mo's boss. He is the very nice man who gave me the false document to self-certify for my flat.

"Hi," he replies, glancing up. "How are you?" Did I detect a certain coolness? Was he thinking, 'Oh no, not that bloody woman wanting another favour.' He would have been right there. I need him to up the fictitious amount of money he paid me so I could give it to Bender the solicitor and get my mortgage for the flat.

"I'm fine," I smile.

"Are you?" he asks. I nod and smile even more. "Good," he replies dismissively, looking back down at his work. Damn! What is the matter with him? Maybe things weren't going so well with the business.

"I've got a bit of a problem," I begin nervously and carry on with my explanation whilst he looks at me with a strange, quizzical expression. I don't care if he despises me, as long as he is prepared to give me what I need.

"I see," he says, leaning back in his chair. "Can I ask you something?"

"Yes. Fire away."

"Are you really alright?"

Was I what? "Why? Do I look ill or something?"

"No," he pauses. "It's just that… when I saw you last, you seemed a bit upset. You ran away from me like I was the devil or something." He gave a snort when he said 'Devil'. "On Primrose Hill. About a week ago. It was early evening."

It's like someone has thrown a bomb into my brain. Everything starts scrambling - memory flipping backwards and forwards, panic rising. "You didn't seem quite with it and, when I went to help you up, you pushed me away and ran off."

"Did I?"

"Are you ok?"

"Ah… yes, yes. Erm… Right. Ah! I remember now. God, I'm sorry. Oh yeah, I'd been for a late boozy lunch - one of my friend's birthdays and you know how it is, it just went on and on and on. Eventually, I left and I thought the best way to sober up was to be out in the fresh air. I think I must have fallen asleep, er… having a nightmare or dreaming or something when you found me… erm..." My voice tails off. He just keeps staring at me. "I don't normally drink like that, honestly. That's probably why I reacted so weirdly. I'm not used to it. Really... I'm not a drinker. I'm actually very…"

"Don't worry." He leans back in his chair. "I believe you and, even if I didn't, it's not a problem Angela. I'll still sort your stuff out for you, give you the raise you need." He winked. "I'll get it written up and let you know when you can pick it up."

"That's great, thanks so much. Sorry if I was rude at the time." I get up to go.

"I'll call you."

"Great. Thanks again."

"Maybe we could meet for a coffee?" That gave me a jolt. I turn back and look at him. He's smiling. He has a nice mouth.

"Ok. Yes," I nod then scurry off as quickly as I can.

I get on the bus to head home and sit on the top. It's always a good place to consider stuff. A bit like meditation; the rocking of the bus, thoughts moving backwards and forwards. It's a good way of sorting problems out and I have a problem now: the business in the park. He bought my lie, but it was so odd. This is the second time I'd thought I had seen Duncan. I swear I recognised his voice. How could I confuse Jack with Duncan? Duncan would be in his late fifties/early sixties now, except he couldn't be because he was dead. Wasn't he?

The wheels on the bus go around and around - it sways and turns, stops, starts and somewhere underneath my thoughts I can hear Patti Smith singing 'Jesus died for somebody's sake but not mine... thick heart of stone, my sins my own they belong to me.'

"Tickets please."

"Erm... 30p please."

"Where are you going?"

"Not sure. 30p's worth if that's ok. You can tell me can't you when my time's up?"

"Yes luv, I'll make a point of runnin' all the way up here just to let you know. Who do you think I am - your personal gofer?"

"If you play your cards-"

"Funny!" She says scowling and jabs the ticket into my hands.

So. Jack. Why had my friend Mo not told me about him before? I mean, apart from being attractive, he has his own company, a great career and he seems kind. No doubt he has his pick of women so why is he putting himself out for me? Someone presses the bell and the bus lurches to a halt next to some hoardings with the British Airways advert. 'Breakfast in Paris, dinner in New York' - 'luggage in Bombay' scrawled at the bottom by someone with time and a spray can on their hands. It takes me a moment, but I realise that's what I need. I need to get away. I need a holiday. My mind needs a break from my life. Buying the flat can wait. I just have to make sure my mother is ok.

"So where is Boney now?" I ask as I tie the ragged roof of Saf down with string. I've plastered the tears in the roof with duct tape to stop it from leaking, which makes her look even worse, but with the roof down, she attains a certain joie de vivre. It's a beautiful bright spring day and I'm taking Mum to see Kipling's house in Sussex. "He's gone back to University. He really was very ill, you know. His left ball was the size of a grapefruit."

"A grapefruit! No, surely, you're exaggerating. A grapefruit, Mum?"

"It was. He could barely walk," she insists. "It was like... like an elephant's, and obviously so painful. I know he always makes a fuss at the slightest sniffle, but this time I could see he was in real agony."

"Blimey, an elephant's grapefruit! You could have hired him out to parties. Sounds grotesque."

"Yes, it was rather. It's doubtful whether he will ever be able to have children. Apparently, an attack of mumps so late in life can render the male sterile."

"Well, that wouldn't be such a bad thing, given his parentage."

"What do you mean by that?" Mum looks at me suspiciously. I'm not diving into those murky waters, not today.

"Joking," I reply, throwing a blanket in the back and starting up the engine.

Dear old Saf starts first time, come rain, come shine, and is now, on certain nights, a bed to a smelly, homeless man. I have to fumigate her in the morning when he's shuffled off, but I know about homeless so

I'm cool about it. Obviously, if he was disrespectful and were to defecate or throw up in her, he'd be out on his arse.

With a practised twist and wrench of the gear stick, we trundle off. We take the back roads and, for the first time in a long while, being in the countryside fills me with joy, its sad associations swept away by the newness of life springing up all around. It's a weekday and there are hardly any cars on the roads and I daydream about how it must have looked before the motorways ruined everything. Mum babbles away over the roar of the engine. She doesn't draw breath but I suppose it's because she lives on her own. In exchange for more skivvying, she now inhabits a damp cottage that sits in the grounds of a large Georgian house - the owner of which is dying of cancer. The cottage is wringing with wet. Knowing full well that even the cockroaches are probably staggering around the kitchen with bronchitis, the woman ignores Mum's pathetic requests for some decent kind of heating and carries on dying, without a conscience, in the lap of luxury. I expect that's why she's got cancer. It's karma. Treating Mum like that means she's probably treated everyone like that all her life, so she's getting a smack from the Bhudda for bad behaviour.

The truth is that most of our sort were brought up in damp, freezing-cold houses and it was completely normal. Rheumatism comes with the territory. When we lived in the old house with Duncan, Sunday afternoons were dedicated to wooding expeditions to feed the insatiable maw of the open fires, which, for two kids was about as much fun as breaking ice in a Siberian gulag with a blunt toothpick; especially with the dictator heading the operations.

Funnily enough, loads of my friends have recently become Buddhists. Someone in the Buddhist camp did a great P.R. job on the greedy Westerners. They've got them all to join up and told them they can chant for whatever they fancy, exonerated from accusations of rampant materialism. Masses have bought into it and are now wailing all times of the day for wealth, status, soul mates... whatever. As a religion, I think it's ok because it's cool about animals but in the end, it's like all religions, it reckons it has the answer to everything.

Mum pulls out a scarf and arranges it like the Queen does, tucking her hair in and tying a double knot under her chin. She shouts, "When I came for an interview for this job, Mrs Cayman said (that's her employer), 'I can't possibly employ you - you're one of us.'" I can tell that this recognition gives her pleasure. Despite the years of poverty, she has hung on to that precious part of her identity she holds so dear. The one that has its roots in the ruling classes.

"How did you get the job then?" I shout back.

"Oh, I had to beg her. I was so desperate and, in the end, she must have felt sorry for me." Not that sorry, I think. Our class never inconvenience themselves enough to tap into their suffocated feelings of empathy. With this lot, there's an unspoken sense that, if you are in trouble, it's probably your own 'jolly fault.'

"I shouldn't tell you this." Mum leans into me conspiratorially. "I had a swig of Mrs Cayman's medicine when she was out of the room the other day. It was extraordinary. You know my back pain vanished almost immediately and I felt absolutely wonderful!"

I slam on the brakes. "You did WHAT?" I asked, turning to her in horror. "Don't tell me you had some of her heroin?"

Mum looks startled. "It's not heroin, it's morphine."

"Heroin/ morphine! Tomatoes/tomaytos! Heroin is a derivative of morphine for God's sake!"

"Is it? Well, I only had a bit. Not so she'd notice," she says defensively.

"But you obviously did! Christ, are you mad? You can't go swigging morphine like that when you've never had it before... or... I... if..."

I'm spluttering with horror. "You shouldn't touch the stuff ever... never... or... at all anyway! Mum, are you mad?"

"Oh, now you're overreacting. I shan't do it again. I just wanted to see what it was like. She told me it stops all her pain and my back has been so awful what with the cleaning and standing for hours cooking."

Now my damn mother is hitting the hard stuff! My reckless mother! 'Ungovernable' was the word Granny called her, sending her off as soon as she could to a convent in Belgium in the hope that the 'brides of Christ' would crush her rebellious nature. Nuns, like horsebreakers, have a pretty solid reputation for doing that sort of work. Obviously, it was only partially successful. Maybe, I think, this is my opportunity to tell her about James and his problem with the stuff. I glance over at her. The shine has gone out of her and I feel horrible. Behind her defensiveness, I can see she's crestfallen. She hates confrontation. I rev Saf up and pull out again into the country lane. "It's alright Mum, I understand your back is awful. It's just really dangerous, that's all."

"I know. I won't do it again," she says apologetically, like a kid that's been caught with your prized Christian Dior lipstick smeared all over its face. That's my whole problem with Mum. She's just like a child. I just can't be hard on her. I smile and tut and she, relieved that we're friendly once more, laughs out loud and bursts into song. "Oh, what a beautiful morning! Oh, what a beautiful day." And it is.

We trundle past sprinklings of purple crocuses under spreading oak trees and swathes of egg yolk yellow daffodils whilst newborn lambs with their bulky mothers speckle the fields. It's real Rupert Brooke stuff and it reminds me of the Shell nature films the headmaster at my prep school used to show on a rainy Sunday in a desperate attempt to occupy his troop of abandoned children.

We drive through a small village, which is remarkable, not because it's particularly picturesque, but because it seems empty, like there has been a terrible plague and the populace is all dead - rotting inside the cottages. "God, this place feels very strange," I say as we pass the local shop that is closed, as is the pub.

"Oh look!" exclaims Mum, pointing at an odd-looking building on the outskirts. "'The House of Pipes.' That's open. Shall we have a look?"

"Pipes, Mum? What about Kipling? You really want to see pipes?"

"Don't you? I think it might be fun."

"Pipes, fun?"

"Well, no, but I thought it might be different."

"Ok, let's see pipes different then." I acquiesce because it is her day.

We park up in the silent street and walk up to the house. Mum grasps the knocker and raps smartly on the fake mediaeval wooden door. She's about to give it another go when it opens suddenly and a large man in his late 40s appears. I know instantly that he is odd. He has a strange, undecided expression, an uncertain smile that struggles to work its way over the smooth, rounded plains of his moon-like face. He completely dwarfs Mum who, looking up, says brightly, "Hello. Are you open?"

Nodding, he steps back and she trots through, followed by a reluctant me trying to work out how I am going to save us before he pushes us into the cellar with the remains of all the other disappeared villagers.

We enter into a dark, eerie hall surrounded by crimson velvet curtaining with an old-fashioned ticket kiosk set back in their folds. Without a word, he disappears through a gap in the drapes. We follow his line of movement by the bulges in the curtains and occasional grunts as he collides into things then, all of a sudden, his face pops up behind the plastic pane of the ticket kiosk. We pay what I think is an exorbitant amount and are instructed to follow the pointing finger saying 'THIS WAY.' I'm hugely relieved to find ourselves coming into a brightly lit room. It has several tall glass cases displaying a vast collection of pipes. Pipes from every era, and every country and, if you were into pipes, you would have been delighted. "Golly," says Mum, trying to sound interested. "Hasn't he got a lot?"

"Far too many," I whisper. "How long do you think we should give it before we can go?" But before I get an answer, the pipe man is upon us and, without further ado, starts in on a history lesson.

I had noticed when buying the tickets there was some sort of problem with his speech, but since he'd hardly said anything, I had dismissed it. I mean what's a remedial 'r' in the greater scheme of things? But neither Mum nor I are prepared for the impediment he has. It's like nothing we'd ever heard before. God knows what was going on in his mouth. Each word is so fantastically distorted it is impossible to make head or tail of what he was saying, but I only once dare look at Mum. She has a gargoyle of a grimace on her face as she tries to hold herself together but I can see, like me, all she wants to do is bellow with laughter. Trying to be polite, she manages to ask him a question, which dissolves into a fake cough. For a blessed moment, he moves away and I manage to whimper, "For God's sake, don't ask any more questions."

"Oh dear, this is too awful," she replies, her voice trailing off into a high-pitched whine as she loses control and fumbles to open her handbag. She thrusts her head into it, scrabbling desperately for a hanky, shoulders beginning to shake. She looks like a horse with a nosebag. I can feel my lips giving way and a strangled cry bursts forth. Laughing when you shouldn't is agony, especially when you know it could be hurtful to someone, but I can't stop myself. I press my face up against one of the glass cases, trying to get a grip on myself and look as if I am fascinated by the array of pipes, but it's hopeless. I splutter and cough and leave a line of drool on the glass.

As soon as he starts up again, I know the game is up. "Got to go to the loo. I'll see you at the car," I manage to blurt out as I speed blindly towards the exit. When she finally catches up with me outside, we lean against the car and yelp with laughter.

"Why?" she guffaws as she hangs on to the wing mirror. "Why didn't his wretched parents get something done about it when he was little? I mean, really! That poor man. It's really too bad. He must have dealt with people like us all his life. I am so ashamed." She blows her nose loudly and dabs away at her tears. "Ah dear," she sighs, trying hard to pull herself together, but one glance at me and we are off again.

I think that was the last time I properly laughed with my mother.

I leave her that evening waving to me from the porch of the mouldy cottage, waving and smiling and I, keeping up the pretence, smiling, and waving back until she is out of sight, whereupon I let out an animal wail of such pain, I shock myself. I'm not usually so bad. How many more times will I have to watch that small figure fading into the distance on someone else's neglected doorstep? How am I ever going to rescue her from her lonely, arduous, miserable life? Where is the sudden and remarkable upturn in fate that people so often speak about; that chance moment that changes everything? Why can't it happen for her, this gentle, romantic little woman who has been so crushed by the successive cruelty of others and their buggered-up wiring? After 5 miles, I have sobbed myself dry and, as the distance lengthens between us, the pain subsides.

The moon bobs in and out behind the trees as it travelled with me and I suddenly realise how little I noticed it now that I live in the city. Here it is, running companionably alongside, lighting up the landscape, reminding me of another life once lived. In my mind's eye, I can see my mother and I, the teenage girl, walking the old Sussex chalk track up the hill to the shepherd's hut, the moon lighting our way, our two cats and dog trotting along in front. We look back down on the farm where our latest home, a grotty little semi-detached tied cottage huddles amongst the dark frosted winter fields. This hovel in exchange for so many hours of cleaning and cooking. Mum bows to the full moon and I, as a typical teenager, wish she wouldn't.

I felt very sorry when Man finally trampled on the moon. Everyone was so excited, but I thought, 'Bang goes another mysterious, beautiful thing under the hobnail boots of Homo sapiens', and I felt sad for days. Fancy sticking a bloody flag on it! And what about Leika the dog the barbaric Russians sent up in a Sputnik? Leika died after a week of going into orbit it turned out, but I didn't know that at the time because, when I first heard about it, I was 7. I suspected something awful had taken place. I didn't want to believe that they had sent a dog into space knowing full well she was being sent to her death. I wanted to think something had gone wrong so I didn't ask the questions like, 'How did Leika get back to Earth? How did she know what buttons to press to come down from outer space? Where is she living now?' I didn't want to ask the questions because something told me I didn't want to know. They showed all these pictures of her with the heading: 'Brave Leika the husky.' In my heart, I knew she wasn't brave. She just didn't know what was going to happen to her. Even at that age, something terrible niggled at the back of my young mind which I sensed would have a huge effect on my perception of the human world unalterably and forever, so I sidestepped it. But a couple of years later, I happened to see, quite by mistake, Richard Dimbleby's TV report on the Belsen concentration camp. The shock was terrible. Not least because those horrifying images meant there was no more escaping the truth. I was forced to confront the reality of the world that I was going to have to live in. There were terrible people out there and what was a dog to these people when you can gas children and grown-ups in their thousands?

Chapter Eight
CHEERS!

1980's

Holiday!

It seemed like a good idea at the time hiding in the hold of the bus until the coach driver shut the door and we heard the lock click. It hadn't occurred to me that there would be no air. It was unnervingly dark in there as well. Nothing was visible, not even the glint of an eyeball. "Can you see my teeth, Mo?" I whispered. I thought my brilliant white caps might pierce the blackness.

"No," came the reply. "And you're crushing my foot."

"Sorry." I tried to fold my body into an even more compact origami shape. A garden gnome minus its fishing rod would have had a hard time squeezing itself into this space, never mind two fully grown women.

"I don't like this. It's really frightening. What if they find us?" whispered Mo.

"It'll be fine," I said, thinking of all the not–so–fine outcomes. "Anyway, what can they do? Hang us? It's not the Second World War, you know. There aren't Nazis out there."

"Bloody feels like it. Why did I listen to you?"

I knew what she meant. I'd had my Anne Frank moment. My greater fear was centred around the coach driver who I had inveigled into giving us a lift back from the South of France where we had ended up camping. If he turned out to be a serial killer/part-time rapist, or just simply forgot to let us out being too tired after having done a 48-hour shift with only an hour's break, no longer in the prime of his life, possibly with a heart condition and – BANG! BANG! BANG! The noise ricocheted round the tiny space. "Oh God! What's going on?"

"Ssssh!" I shushed but I could feel the panic rising and my heart sprinting. French voices could be heard outside and then more BANG! BANG! BANG! "It must be the customs men," I whispered.

"What shall we do?"

As I considered the options, the voices began to recede and the banging became more distant as they moved round to inspect the other side of the coach. We listened to our hearts thumping in the silence. "How much air do you think we would need to survive if the driver doesn't let us out until we reach London?" asked Mo.

"Just enough for me, but unfortunately, you have the larger nostrils."

"Funny," she hissed. The sound of another door banging and then the reassuring tremble and shake as the engine started up and the coach lumbered forward.

It seemed like ages before we heard the last car door slam and the ferry began to rock as we sailed out of port and, to be honest, that's when I properly began to panic, though I kept it to myself since it was me who had got us into the situation. The thing was, if it did end up happily ever after, I could dine out on the escapade for weeks but on the other hand, ending up dead wasn't such a brilliant thing. Suddenly, there was a knocking on the door and light flooded in as the coach driver pulled it open. "Allo girls. You alright in there?" I didn't bother to answer. I bolted headfirst, almost knocking him over in my rush to get out. Minutes later, we were upstairs with tea and toast in the cafe, all at the poor bloke's expense as we had about 10p between us. It had to be said that he was very kind helping us out as he did. He even dropped us off at Westminster Bridge which was pretty decent of him.

Back in Blighty, nothing had changed. Mum hadn't been miraculously lifted out of poverty and by all accounts James was... well I don't know about James and I didn't know why I thought my being away for a week would have some mystical effect on all things that were causing me grief, but holidays could make you feel like that. I was energised after my time with sea and sun and I used it quickly before it ran out to ring up my acting agent, sounding bright and go-getty.

"Oh hi there, it's Angela, just rung to say I'm back, and-"

"Sorry, who?"

"Angela. Angela Fleming."

"Can you hold on please?" came the weary response followed by a clatter as the phone dropped onto a desk. I waited, hoping against hope she was sifting through times and dates of auditions for me. Eventually, I had to shout, "Is anyone there?" several times, until eventually the assistant picked up and said hesitantly, "Hello," as if she were going to find some weirdo on the other end. "Oh, it's you. Hold on, I'll pass you over."

"It's very quiet," said my agent, as if she really cared, and gave me my few seconds of commiseration that agents generally built into their conversation with actors who were out of work, then put the phone down. I was beginning to rue the day I'd ever been a mole.

I rang around the promotions agencies and came away with a gig that night for a Dutch lager in a pub in

Canning Town (where?) with the possibility of performing at a night club in Streatham as the fourth member of another human fruit machine sometime in the future. Fired up by such resounding results, I felt I should push forward on the flat thing and ring Jack to see if he had got my fake wage rise sorted. I had decided after much contemplation, during the long coach journey back from France, that I should just ignore the incident in the park and play it as if nothing had happened.

He wasn't in.

I left a message.

In the dark and rain, it took Saf and I hours to find Canning Town. When I did, it was as if the place had been kicked under a stone and forgotten about. Saf, her one windscreen wiper working overtime, rattled across the potholed road towards the grim and grubby-looking pub which stood in what had been a bombed-out area. There was a scattering of houses nearby and, in the distance, a couple of tower blocks but other than that, no sign of life and only the smallest bit of street lighting. My heart sank. In my ignorance, I presumed Canning Town was just another suburban sprawl, somewhere innocuous like Merton.

The comedy aspect of putting a Dutch cap on in a pub lavatory wasn't lost on me as I looked at myself in the mirror. I was in full Dutch girl costume; ludicrous hat and clogs, the whole gouda cheese shebang, and I was about to go out into a room where no female, except for the hard-nosed barmaid and I presume, a percentage of unseen vermin, ever ventured. My task – and I believe Heracles had easier ones – was to promote the lager by engaging the hard-drinking, monosyllabic males who populated this drinking hole into playing childish party games; the sort of games someone in rehab from a severe stroke could master.

Anything but a party atmosphere was happening in this drab, forlorn place. I must have seemed like an explosion of colour when I clogged my way through the loo doors in my green dress, crisp white cap and pinny. Not that anyone bothered to turn or look, but then I knew straight away these were the sort of men who saw everything through the back of their necks.

I set up my ridiculous little shove halfpenny board and the electric wire job which you have to get the loop along without touching and waited. And I waited. The barmaid looked at me like I was something she had never been exposed to before. I had a go on the electric thingy and realised after hanging around for what seemed an age that nobody was going to approach me so I would have to go to them. Taking a deep breath, I clogged my way over to one of the unseeing/seeing men silently drinking at the bar. "Excuse me. Would you like to have a go on one of the games and get yourself a free lager?" My smile was actually hurting my ears, it was so jaw-bracingly wide. Slowly, he turned and looked at the voucher I was holding. He stared at it for a moment, then shook his head and turned back. The barmaid was hypnotised. I looked down the bar. Her gaze followed mine. Two rough-looking men sat on the stools. She looked back at me. Her expression signalled, 'I wouldn't bother if I was you.' I had no choice. A fatal stabbing would have been better than an evening of such intense boredom. Even when her expression flashed, 'Stupid cow, be told!' I continued to move towards them. "Hello, can I interest you in-"

"Is that a Dutch cap?" Smirks and snorts.

“Yes, and this is a traditional Dutch costume. Perhaps you would like to try our traditional Dutch games and…”

"You come from up west, do ya?"

"Yes. Yes, I do.”

"Not 'Olland then?"

"No. Not Holland." I shook my head. "You think I'd come all the way from Holland to do this?" They laughed then turned their backs and carried on snorting and grunting at one another. I clattered off across the wooden floor, back to my post, wondering how the hell I was going to last another 4 glacial hours. After tinkering with the games, going to the loo and trying hard to avoid eye contact with the barmaid who continued to stare at me like an unblinking owl, I decided the only way through was to have a drink. I’d dip into the pathetic sum I was going to be paid and in future, refuse to go anywhere east again. I walked up to the bar. “May I have a vodka and lime please with ice?” She nodded, uncrossed her arms and, resting her fag in the ashtray, went about the business. I looked down at my watch. I wondered how many vodkas I could stretch to before I knocked off or was knocked out.

“Here you are luv.” The barmaid pushed the drink towards me.

“Oh no, sorry. I didn’t ask for a double.”

“Someone’s buying for you,” she said flatly.

That came as an unnerving surprise. My eyes swept the room. Which one of those disinterested backs had done this?

“Oh, how kind,” I lied. “Who should I thank?”

“Nah,” she replied, picking up the fag, taking a drag, then exhaling deeply. "They don't want to say.”

Weird and worrying, I sipped my drink and tried not to look any further than two inches in front of me. As the hour dragged by, more and more vodkas and lime began to line up at the end of the bar. "These are for you luv," the barmaid indicated with a nod of her head as their ranks swelled.

"Oh my God," I replied. "I can't drink all these. I have to drive home. I think you better tell the person who is doing this to stop."

"If I do, will you let me play with your toys?"

I looked round into the smiling face of... Jack! I nearly bit a hole in my glass.

He laughed with that nice mouth of his.

"What are you doing here?" I spluttered. Surprise and pleasure curdled with paranoia as I tried to take in his presence.

"I got your message and Mo told me you were working here, so I thought I would hand deliver your pay rise." He held out an envelope. "Also, I wanted to see what a 'producer' does when she's moonlighting!"

"Did you follow me here?"

"No. Why?" he replied, his smile fading.

He was probably thinking I was about to go loopy on him again, but let's face it, I wasn't about to bolt off through the bleak streets of Canning Town on a winter's night dressed as a Dutch peasant. "No reason. It's just... you know... a bit of a shock and this place is in the back of beyond."

"Yeah, you can say that again."

"You must have been here for a while. Why didn't you come over?"

"Didn't like to. You were working."

"Yeah, rushed off my clogs."

He laughed again. "Come on, I'll play you at shove halfpenny. I get a free beer don't I if I win?"

"Yes. Yes, you do," I said, smiling back at him.

"I bought the flat."

"Darling, how wonderful!"

"I know, Mum, can you believe it? Mr Bender got me a mortgage. You can stay here whenever you want, you know. I'm sharing it with Jonathan," I enthused.

"How lovely. Is that gay Jay?"

"Yes. Gay Jay. We just have to raise some money to get the boiler out of the garden shed. Skint at the moment. I'm only making enough to pay the mortgage."

"Of course."

There was a pause.

"You ok?" I could tell by her forced enthusiasm she wasn't but sort of hoped she might keep it to herself.

"Bit concerned. I have to move from this place as Mrs Cayman has finally died. Poor thing."

"Oh no. Have you got somewhere else?" I felt my heart sinking.

"Nothing as yet. There's almost nothing in situations vacant of The Lady. Plus, James is in a bit of trouble."

"Again?" I asked.

"Oh look, I don't want to worry you."

"No, go on."

"Well, he's had a bit of an accident in the car."

"Your Skoda?"

"Yes. I'm afraid so. He swears he hadn't touched a drop, and I believe him, but the police breathalysed him and he was over the limit. James says they fiddled it."

'He would, wouldn't he?' I thought. "Is the car alright?"

"No. It's a write-off. I'm going to have to find another one, but it'll have to be an old banger again as I don't have enough money to buy something as nice as the Skoda. Of course, I won't get any insurance."

"Have you got anything left of Granny's money?"

"About £3,000. As you know, there wasn't very much."

"Yes. That's why you shouldn't keep blowing it on my brother." I could feel the fury scorching up through my body like a fireball. What was wrong with my mother? Why did she continue to delude herself about James? Of course, I knew why - but why did I have to hear it, deal with it, put up with it? In that instant, I had had enough of all the romantic, delusory crap she had foisted on us all her life. I took a deep breath. "Look Mum, I think it's time to go to the council and put yourself down for a council flat."

There was a fat silence.

The pretence of saying as she always said at the end of yet another desperate crisis, 'Ah well, one day our ship will come in,' those times were over. Her ship had sunk long ago and she had to accept it was only me on the life raft, paddling furiously, who had any hope of dragging her and my brother out of the choppy waters. "No Angela, I cannot do that. You know that," came the reply.

"It would only have to be temporary until something better turned up. At least it's a place for your furniture. Think about it just as a stop-gap that's all." Another silence as upbringing and reality fought it out. "Mum, you can't keep working as a cook and a skivvy with your back and you can't keep being moved on. You're getting too old for all this. Your back is terrible. You have got to be sensible."

“Council places were not meant for us, Angela. We have no right to them. They are for the poor working class.”

“Well, you are now.”

“You know what I mean,” she sighed. “That aside, I’ll never live it down. Can you imagine what my sister would think?”

“I know, but listen. When I get some money, I’m sure we’ll find you somewhere nice to live, I promise, meanwhile, we are dealing with your survival. Look at it like that.” Another silence. "Mum?”

“I’ll think about it. I have to go.”

“I can ring the council for you, or come with you whatever you ne–“

“Darling, I have to go. I’ll call you. Bye.” She was gone.

I put the phone down and thought about all those places we had been moved on from and felt almost guilty that I had managed to find somewhere myself.

Chapter Nine
GOD REST YOU MERRY GENTLEMEN

It was Christmas. Our mother's last Christmas in the private sector. She had finally accepted her fate and was about to move into a council flat but with the little money she had left, she'd insisted on renting a month's worth of a private house where she could pretend it was her own which appealed to her sense of beauty.

The property was a Georgian cottage in an unkempt garden surrounded by ancient apple trees with twisted lichen-covered branches, backing onto open fields. The place must have lain empty for ages because the dead owl I had to remove from my fireplace was only recognisable by the unusually large holes that had been its eyes. As usual, there was no heating apart from open fires. To Jack and my two other London friends, Chris and Fran, who I had bravely invited to stay, it was an adventure. To Boney and myself, it was the same old same old; pretty from the outside, damp and cold inside, with dishevelled-looking furniture that Mum had attempted to detract from by decorating the place with holly and ivy, along with a few of her belongings – a couple of pictures, some cushions and photos of us as kids on the mantelpiece. I hadn't seen Boney for ages. "Darling, don't for goodness sake bring up his testicles will you?" cautioned Mum.

"My brother's testicles are not a topic of conversation I want to explore, so please don't worry yourself on that count."

"Don't be unkind," she said with a winsome look.

"I'm not. I'm his sister. He's my brother. We don't discuss our genitalia."

"No. Well, I'm just saying. He's very sensitive about them."

"Aren't most men?" I countered. "If men had the same feeling for women and other species as they do about their balls, we would all be living in a kind of paradise don't you think?"

"Possibly," she laughed. "Anyway, just to let you know, he went off to visit his father's other family last week."

"Other family?" I asked, sitting up like a dog that'd just heard the word W.A.L.K. "You mean Duncan's children from his-"

"Yes," Mum cut in quickly. I was never sure whether she felt guilty about being the 'other' woman or whether she resented Duncan's former wife and kids. Certainly, they were never mentioned as if the subject was taboo. They hung in our consciousness like shadowy figures in an old oil painting, brush stroked over by the artist; once favoured, now supplanted, their partial forms half-glimpsed beneath the oils. "Right, I really must start getting the supper ready." She headed towards the kitchen. "Can you be an angel and get some wood in from the woodshed and stoke up the fire?"

'Well-dodged Mum,' I thought as she disappeared off.

So, Boney had sought out his half-siblings, the ones we never met, the ones never spoken about, the ones my stepfather had abandoned in order to persecute us. I really wanted to know about them. Had he treated them like us? Was he just a monster through and through? "Hey Boney, why don't you and I walk down to the pub and pick up some beers for supper?" I said as he mooched into the room with a wedge of cheese in one hand and a bag of crisps in the other. He'd already raided the kitchen in typical half-starved student fashion, only he wasn't a student anymore. He'd finished studying PPE that summer at Exeter Uni. "My shout," I said, knowing that would be irresistible to him.

"Yeah, ok," he said, shovelling the rest of the cheese in his mouth.

I put my head around the door of the sitting room where my friends lolled in front of the open fire, their faces rosy with the heat. "Won't be long," I said. "Just getting some booze in."

The cold air hit as soon as we stepped outside. We followed the dark, narrow back lane which resembled an Arthur Rackham drawing, twisting into the night, the roots of trees running like old, contorted veins along the high banks. Once a track, it was now worn deep into the earth by the footfall of people and animals over the years. It had a silence of its own as if aided and abetted by the overhanging canopy of branches that curled over our heads, keeping the light out and the silence in. My voice sounded unnaturally loud as I turned to Boney and asked as nonchalantly as I could, "So, what have you been up to?"

"Errm… Not a lot," he replied. "You haven't got a fag have you?"

"Not on me. Some back at the house."

"Tsk."

"Didn't you go travelling or something?" I asked, hoping to jog him.

"Travelling? Well… wouldn't call it that."

"Mum said you'd been driving round England," I insisted.

"I wouldn't call it 'driving' either, not in that old banger. More like pushing it round England. The bloody thing kept breaking down. It's had it really but the

M.O.T. doesn't expire until February and it won't pass another, so I want to keep it going until then."

"Ahh. But you stayed with friends on your journey?"

"Yeah. Couple. Saw my ex from school. Glad we split up. She's a punk now with a baby and a habit."

"Sad."

"Yeah. Sad."

"Who else?" I asked.

"Erm... Neil from school. He's moved to Nottingham. He was working for the council and... Jesus it's cold, come on." Seeing the light of the pub glowing a bruised yellow in the distance, he broke into a run.

The latch of the pub door made the familiar click as we stepped into the cosiness of the public bar. Boney positioned himself against the counter, casting a cursory glance round the room and said casually, "I met my other half-brothers and sister last summer," just as the barman came over and asked, "What can I get you?"

Damn!

"What?" I said.

"Think we want some lagers to take away don't we?" replied Boney.

'Er yes. Eight cans of Stella, please."

"Right you are," smiled the barman.

"Got to go for a waz," said Boney and disappeared off to the gents.

"What's this, having a sneaky one without us?" shouted Jack, appearing in the doorway as Fran and Chris bundled in behind him.

Back at the cottage, I'd managed to get Boney into the kitchen alone and it had only needed a gentle nudge on the subject and he was ready to spout.

"Justin, the son, is an academic and Mary, his sister, is a florist. Their mum died from an asthma attack a couple of years ago." Boney was putting the cans of beer into the fridge whilst eating his way through a bag of pork scratchings.

"How were they?" I asked

"Want some?" He rattled the scratchings packet at me. I shook my head.

"Where do they live?"

"Lincolnshire. About 5 miles away from each other. They seem to be quite close."

"They weren't at Duncan's funeral - you know that don't you?"

"Yeah, well."

"They don't think he's still alive, do they?"

"Course not. Why would they think that?"

"Dunno. Only... people like him don't die."

"Don't be ridiculous and, by the way, he was my father."

"Not your fault."

"Anyway, they had nothing much to say about him, but then they didn't put the boot in either."

"Really? I am surprised. When was the last time they saw him?" I asked.

"Don't know. They are actually very nice, very ordinary, gentle people. Not especially fucked up like us-"

"Speak for yourself! I'm not fucked up!"

He pulled a face. "I am NOT fucked up," I repeated.

"Well, James most certainly is-"

"What's that about James? Is he coming to join us? Have you seen him, Boney?" Mum appeared at the mention of James' name, as if beckoned by some invisible force.

"No, Mum and no, Mum." Boney was as defeated as I was about our mother's situation, but he kept away from it as best he could. He had stronger emotional armour than me, maybe because he'd had Mum's undivided attention as a kid, only having to share it in the holidays when James and I were back from our respective prisons. By the time he was 7, we were both gone. Being the only child, it seems, made you naturally and unapologetically selfish, which I wished I was, instead of which I resent it in others.

"Oh, that's a shame. It would be so lovely to have you all together. It's so sad he isn't here," Mum sighed wistfully.

I had to remove myself then. It always came down to James. Pissed me off. Pissed me off that I was never enough. Here I was, making the grand gesture by inviting my friends down so she could have a fun, noisy, happy Christmas - exposing myself as I unveiled the truth about my lack of a parental home and a mother living on almost nothing - to people who had both; risking something that not long ago would have been unthinkable and could have put me right outside the boundaries of my new herd and all she could do was sigh about James.

In spite of that, it was a Christmas to remember. We all sat round a turkey that we had to saw away at with someone's Swiss army knife as none had been provided by the owner of the cottage. Two of us had to perch on an upturned crate and a laundry basket while the rest sat on rickety chairs gathered around an old scarred wooden dining table. We drank champagne out of teacups and plastic tumblers and laughed a lot. Mum, flushed rosy pink with alcohol, sat back in her chair and watched us with smiling curiosity; this other generation, easy with their ways and generous in their inclusion.

We flew a kite in the biting cold wind out in the fields at the back. The land was monochrome in the grey, drabness of winter. The fields, lifeless and trees skinned of their leaves, looked like thorns on the horizon. We watched the kite flap and twist then nosedive to the ground as if the torment of flight was too much for it. I did think of James then and felt sad. Sad and angry, but mostly sad. It was the countryside prodding me again, reminding me, asking me, 'Where is he? Your brother? Why isn't he with you?' I retreated back into the cottage where memory didn't reside and stoked up the fire.

"Don't forget, Aunt Maddie is coming over at four." A groan went up from Boney and me. "Don't be like that," she admonished. "She's bringing your presents and she won't stay long. I just hope she doesn't bring her frightful lover, Hugo Scragg, with her."

"So do I. Anyway, I thought you weren't talking," I replied.

"Well, you know what she's like. She keeps on and on at me until I have to give in."

"Actually, you don't have to, but why would she bring him? She knows you can't stand him."

"Because he's her slave. She doesn't move without him these days. Apparently, he's so smitten, she caught him training his binoculars on her from the bedroom window when she takes the dog for a walk."

"What? Whose bedroom window?" I asked.

"His. She's got him in the garage now."

I looked perplexed. "You know that poky little flat above the garage," she explained.

"She's stuffed him in there has she?"

"Yes. "

"And has she?" asked Boney.

"Oh really, don't be foul. I wouldn't know, nor would I want to."

"Me neither. What about Uncle StJohn?" I said.

"I think StJohn probably sees him as a blessing. It means he gets time off from her constant demands. You know StJohn, he's only really interested in horse racing, cricket and whisky."

"I thought they had a good marriage."

"Well, they probably do now, as Scragg takes up the slack, though I think having to share your wedding anniversary, Christmas, birthdays et al with the lover may become a little trying. Scragg is a dreadful little bore. StJohn has nothing in common with him-"

"Apart from his wife's vagina."

"Boney, really! That's revolting! She is after all your aunt you know. I'm well aware she's coming here to gloat and it's so humiliating, but it is Christmas after all."

Aunt Maddie had no natural talents herself but was fiercely competitive. Her fairy godmother had done well by her. With one wave of her fairy wand, it seems she bestowed upon her shamelessness, selfishness and ruthless determination – this being the cocktail that humans need to succeed in this world. Mum's fairy godmother on the other hand, must have been absent, either that or had taken her eye off the ball. Attributes such as being a good artist, piano player, rider and skater were not sufficient. It might have occurred to it that some mediocre parenting/relationship skills might have been useful along with a bullshit detector for men.

"Darling, how quaint! Where did you find this?" Aunt Maddie arrived bearing gifts as if dispensing charity to the impoverished workers. She was tall, head and shoulders above her older sibling, and wrapped in a cashmere coat with a fur collar. "Oh, honestly, you are funny Helen. I mean, where did you get the money to rent this? Surely you can't afford it?" she exclaimed, walking into the house like a glamorous film star – all perfume, red lipstick and (yet more) fur-lined boots.

Interesting how wealthy people insist the poor should never waste a penny on anything that could remotely pull them out of their hard-pressed life for a few days; profligacy being their preserve. Mum mumbled something in response as we both raised our eyes heavenwards and followed in her scented wake as she pushed her way through into the sitting room where my friends stretched out on the floor playing Trivial Pursuit. "Oh I say, look at all these bodies. Are you all tribal creatures?" she cried in mock amazement.

My friends scrambled apologetically to their feet. "My tribe is from an area of North West London," replied Jack, extending his hand and smiling broadly. "Where's yours?"

"Hampshire," she answered, as if she owned the entire county.

"Naturally," said Jack.

"Tell me," she said, parking herself in the only armchair. "Do you use furniture where you come from?"

"Occasionally," he replied, adopting a squatting position whilst the rest of us managed to squeeze ourselves on the sofa and an upturned packing case.

"Goodness," she laughed. "Are you sure you aren't related to the American Indian - isn't that how they sit?"

"Not as far as I know. But yes, I do like to squat every now and then. It's a great position for mulling things over and, of course, it's the optimum position to adopt when defecating as it enables the colon to evacuate effectively."

"Really?" she replied, her smile souring fractionally. "That would make a good topic at dinner parties. Obviously not the sort I would go to." Without missing a beat, she turned to Mum. "Darling, do open the presents I brought. I can't stay as we've got the Sandersons coming tonight and I've got to get back to make sure the cook knows exactly what's what. Not only that, we went 'beagling' this morning, which was great fun, but after all that walking, I must get a bath in." I avoided commenting on the barbaric sport of 'beagling', not wanting to upset the apple cart. Mum obediently pulled the bag of presents towards her and doled them out whilst my friends looked on, fascinated. I got a woolly scarf and hat, worthy of an Enid Blyton character. Boney got a book of interesting facts, the sort you read in the lavatory and poor Mum got a hideous-looking coffee pot and a 'pet stone'. The 'pet stone', even for my aunt, was groundbreaking in its awfulness. The insensitivity of being given a large stone with a string attached for a lead was lost on my aunt. This was the frivolity of the stupid rich, their trite humour expertly exploited by some jerk in the manufacturing world. "Isn't it just the funniest thing? I mean when I saw it, I nearly died laughing. And darling, it's got instructions!" Aunt Maddy scrabbled excitedly in the box, her gold bracelets and diamonds glinting and jangling as she searched. "Ah! Here they are! Do look. It tells you how to take it for a walk, how to care for it and of course, no need to feed it, so very cheap to keep. Perfect for you, Helen. Hilarious don't you think?" Mum managed a crooked smile. My friends looked on mystified.

I did a sort of strangled snort that turned into, "Everyone want tea? I'll put on the kettle."

"Oh no, not for me darling, this is only a flying visit. I must be off," said my aunt, throwing the stone to one side. "Now come here, little Angela, give your aunt a kiss."

"I'm not actually that little. I'm 5 foot 8 now," I muttered defiantly as if my height was some kind of weapon.

"Of course you are," she replied as if pacifying a truculent 12-year-old. She pulled me to her and wrapped me in a bear hug, squashing my face into her perfumed neck where I got a mouthful of dead animal and my eye speared by an earring. "Boney!" she commanded after releasing me. "Come and see me out. I want to hear all about your testicles before I go, but you'll have to make it quick darling as I must rush. Helen, I'll ring you tomorrow."

"Hold on, what about our presents for you and Uncle St John?" Mum asked. "I've got them in the dining room. I've had to get the children a shared present I'm afraid, things being as they are."

"They will be thrilled. Thank you." Somehow, I doubted it. I was quite sure a tin of Quality Street would have been lost amongst the new sports car, gold jewellery and other fabulous presents they'd unwrapped earlier. "Lovely to meet you." She waved to my friends who, strangely, had all lined up and looked as if they were about to salute. "Enjoy the rest of your Christmas and, Jack, do try sitting in the armchair, I think you'll find it's very pleasant and so much better for one's back and knees. Come on, Boney." Boney followed her out sheepishly.

Mum picked up the 'pet stone' and took it into the kitchen where she flung it out of the window. "What a bloody outrage that woman is! I cannot believe she is my sister. I'll give her a pet stone! She's lucky I didn't put it through her car window!" She slammed the window shut. With that, I knew the iron curtain had descended once more on Aunt Maddie – at least for the foreseeable future.

"God's sake, Mum! Did you really have to tell her about my balls?" exploded Boney, appearing in the doorway.

Ah! Christmas. God rest you, merry gentlemen…

The dark was coming in.

Chapter Ten
RED, RED WINE

Christmas has come and gone. The monochrome world of January has set in.

I pull out my jewellery box and climb into bed: the Venetian leather box that once belonged to my grandmother in Edinburgh, where Robert Louis Stevenson was born (his museum filled the dark rooms upstairs). We were banished there for most of the summer holidays. Granny complained, quite rightly, on our final visit, that we behaved like feral rats when she discovered that we had stolen her diamond earrings and other pieces of her jewellery and hawked them around Edinburgh, attempting, to sell them (guess who's idea that was). When she subsequently discovered that her Ming vases and silver coffee pots were stuffed full of rotting food we hadn't wanted, she'd had enough. By the time we left the house, it was almost on the run, it stank so badly. By the age of 9, we were persona non-gratis, which was a relief as far as we were concerned. Not because we didn't like her. We loved her. But it was miserable up there and, in hindsight, I can say we were, by this time, pretty disturbed. Our behaviour was dictated by James who liked anything that had a mildly criminal edge to it. I say mildly because, at this age, it was mostly practised on his close family. I simply went along with it. As my understanding of the world and its inhabitants had left me thinking that humans, apart from my mum and dad, were no more feeling than a wardrobe, why should I care? I was a passive accomplice.

Lifting the lid of the box, the last of cold light glitters its final parting through a tear in the grey clouds outside, catching the glass earrings and throwing a prism of rainbow light onto the wall. Earring lies next to earring, brooch with brooch, cushioned on the worn wine-red coloured velvet. The wine-red velvet dissolves into wine-red water, turning a sticky rust-brown as James bellows in torment and slashes himself again with one swift movement.

The elderly woman crashes through the door, flinging her arms out to him, crying out, leaning over the bath edge, her frail frame tensing like a thin rod of iron as she tries to haul him out of the water, out of the pain, calling to him, hushing and shushing him.

Her back now in spasm, the worn muscles giving away, she holds on, drawing on every fibre in her body.

'Pull him out, your little boy – no longer a boy in stature but forever a boy at heart.

Pull him out,

hold him to your breast.

Rock him,

rock him like you once did,

but know that no amount of rocking now, can still the pain and stop the horror.'

I try to shake the image out of my head but it keeps replaying itself. I murmur to myself over and over like a mantra. 'It's ok, James is still alive, still alive, still alive."

I close the lid on the box that hails from a world disappeared. One where our inchoate, feral behaviour was the symptom of distress which had now found full expression in James's self-harming, lying in a bath marinating in his own blood; my anguished mother trying to haul him out.

Climbing out of bed, I stand in front of the mirror. I'm wearing an air hostess uniform. I stare at myself for a long time. I hope, if I look long enough, I might see a sign, something to tell me. Tell me what? Was it because of those bad things we did, like stealing, that the world hated us? No. The world hated us before we did anything bad. How else did someone like Duncan come into our lives? If the world hates us anyway, then we can be as bad as we like, but being bad won't stop it from hating us, which means we are doomed and we will never get out of this, it will just go on and on until we die. No matter how many times I run through this, the answer is always the same.

I unpin my air hostess hat, which sits askew on my head, then take off the jacket and let it drop to the floor. The phone rings. "Angela, is that you? What are you doing? The air hostess demo to music starts in half an hour. You were booked on the stand-"

"Yes, sorry," I interrupt. "I'm ill. You'll have to get someone else. Can't talk." I put the phone down, then leave it off the hook. I drag a chair over to the wardrobe and climbing onto it, reach up and pull down a large cardboard box. Opening it, I pull out a small cushion, several scarves, then my searching fingers close upon something soft and furry. I find what I am looking for. Clutching my old teddy bear close to my chest, I climb back into bed.

My bear is here again to comfort me, like he had been all those lonely years at boarding school and when we ran away from Duncan and when my dad disappeared. Good old Bear.

Chapter Eleven
FU MAN CHU

1980'S

I am lying on my back on the thickest, softest carpet I have ever known. One of my cats is lying by my side and we have our legs up, resting against large burr oak double doors. He likes to lie like this and so do I. Helps my back. Once in a while, he farts. I know it's him because it's not me, which is unusual, as I have become allergic to everything it seems, so I am constantly filling up with gas. Also, his farts smell sour. You never hear cats blowing off. Their physical design precludes it because apparently, they don't tighten up so there is a wider channel for the air to pass through. If you can manage to pull your cheeks apart when expelling a 'wind biscuit', as James calls them, there shouldn't be a sound, but your hand scrabbling surreptitiously around your backside, in a room full of people without being noticed, is pretty impossible.

I turn my head and look at my cat. His front paws are curled up loosely under his fat little chin like a cartoon rabbit and his eyes are small slits watching me. His little body vibrates as he purrs. Life is good and this place is like heaven. It's light and spacious and warm. I have 2 cats now and we often just roll around on the carpet because there's no point in getting into a chair or the sofa. Sometimes, I lie face down, spread-eagled on the soft pile, and breathe in because it reminds me of the lovely house we lived in briefly when I was a child with my dad. Just like it was then, everything here is new, modern, and light and the boiler is indoors and its pipes aren't heating the grass as they wound their way through the garden. I sold that first flat with the primitive heating system and bought this one with Jack.

So, here I am in my thirties. Wasn't too much of a hassle leaving my 20s. Mum says a woman comes into her own in her 30s and, for once, she's right. All us women are walking around with great big shoulder pads like American footballers, trying to be dynamic superwomen as promulgated by Shirley Conran. These are good times. No these are wonderful times. Having cats again, having animals in my life makes me realise how empty it has been. Jack likes cats too. He's a good man.

"Angela! La-La! The car's ready, you need to bring the rest of the food down!"

"O.k. Josh, coming."

Josh is my assistant cook. I run my own catering business now to supplement my acting which comes and goes. Josh is Canadian. He has a body like an athlete and the emotional fortitude of a possum. He hasn't trained as a chef - neither have I - but we both love eating and needs must. We work well together. Today, we are off to cook for this dragon of a woman in Kensington Church Street. I've only met her once and she's a bit strange. Her nails are as long as a Mandarin's from the Ming Dynasty and, actually, if she didn't shave, she'd probably have a beard and moustache to match. Despite her affinity with Fu Man Chu, she hails from that dark corner of the map, Eastern Europe, and has bagged herself an English Lord.

At her house, we ring the bell and wait. Eventually, the door is opened by a vision in fuchsia pink. She has shoehorned herself into a silk dress which wrinkles up around her groaning midriff. Her dyed black hair is spun into a walnut whip on top of her head and her heavily made-up face, with eyebrows like grip handles in a disabled lavatory, shows no sign of pleasure. 'This doesn't bode well,' I think. Most hostesses are usually so relieved you actually turn up that they welcome you over the threshold like some foreign potentate, then hang around the kitchen, regaling you with the troubles of their life – their battle with fatty deposits, their bed-wetting kids, their stressed-out husbands, whilst all the while they poke their fingers into the food, making irritating remarks like, "Oh how interesting, I've never seen it made like that before."

"Who is dis?" the vision in pink asks, flicking her liver-spotted claw at Josh.

"This is Josh, my assistant," I reply.

"Hi," he says, smiling warmly, and offers his hand. She gives it a limp shake, scanning him suspiciously with her black eyes, then ushers us into a dark hallway, past an equally dark room where heavy brown furniture can be seen dimly through a chink of light escaping between the velvet drapes. It gets even darker as we are taken down more stairs, past a funereal-looking dining room and into the bowels of the basement where bats would be happy to hang out.

'This place is like Gormenghast," I whisper to Josh just as 'Flay' appears in the guise of His Lordship. Thin, knee-cracking and almost dead, he barely registers our presence as he silently side-steps out of our path as his wife leads us into the kitchen. Unlike Gormenghast, the kitchen is a modest affair i.e. pokey. If the old adage 'Home is where the hearth is', you'd be considered homeless. This wants knocking down and then sprayed with something on the level of Chornobyl just to keep the hostile bacteria under control. The stove, circa

1956, is covered in baked-on grime circa 1956, and there was evidence of unsavoury activity everywhere. Josh and I exchange glances of horror mixed with panic.

"So you use dis back door to bring your tings in. I don't vant you upstairs. No," she says, nodding at me. "Only de man must come in de dining room. It's a very important dinner party with de ambassador of Uruguay as de main guest, so you lady," she jabs a blood-red painted talon at me, "You stay in de kitchen, out of de way."

"Yes, well, that won't be difficult as I will be cooking," I respond tightly.

She ignores me and picks up a small handbell from the side table and rings it vigorously. "When you hear dis bell, you boy come immediately into de dining room and straight to me you understand?"

Josh nods. "I don't vant butter on de table. We use only dis." She jimmies open the fridge door with her claw and pulls out a tub of margarine. "I vant it in rolls like you see in de top restaurants. You know vhat I mean." Has any cook ever been asked to make round curls out of sloppy margarine that doesn't hold its shape? I should have asked to borrow one of her talons - maybe that's what she uses. "I leave you now. We eat at 8 o'clock," she says, peremptorily and waddles off into the darkness.

"La-La, this place is horrible. It's like a freaking morgue," whimpers Josh. "I don't wanna go in that dining room alone with her. She's a vampire, you can tell. She's sucked all the blood out of the old Lord, that's why he's so grey. I know it."

"You don't have to worry, she can see you're gay. She's not going to be doing any sucking." I stare at the grubby cooker and wonder what I can use other than a pick ax to remove the baked-on grime.

"She's not after my cock, she's after my blood. Prime Canadian blood!"

"Well, I'll cook the lamb nice and rare and she can suck on that. Ok?"

"Oh God," he moans as he picks up a sponge to wipe down the surfaces. "This place should be condemned. It's filthy."

"Listen, stop whining and get on with it. We don't have much time and I'm going to have to get some of this dirt off before – Oh Christ, no!" I reel back in horror as I open the oven door and catch sight of something lying on its side.

"What? What is it?" squeals Josh.

"I don't know. Have a look."

Nervously, he inches over and peers in. The piercing shriek he lets out as he jumps back, clapping his hands over his mouth, must have ricocheted down the hall and up the stairs. "Ssh! Ssh! Keep it down." I wave my hands at him.

"Oh my God! No! No! No!" He starts jigging up and down on the spot. "What is it? Oh God, what is it?"

"I don't know. I... I think it might be..."

"What?"

"A dead rat."

"A dead rat! No!"

'Sssh!" I hiss. "They'll hear you."

"Please, please, La-La don't do this."

"I'm not doing anything."

"Shut the oven door for Chrissakes."

"It's not going to jump out. It's dead."

"It's gonna have fleas. They aren't dead. I'm starting to itch. I am. I'm itching all over." He begins scratching himself frantically.

"You're getting hysterical!"

"I swear they've jumped me already. They must have been waiting for someone to open the freaking door."

"Right. That's it. We need to-"

"We? No! Not me. You're on your own," he says, backing out of the room. "And anyways, you can't use the oven after that thing has been in it."

"I have to. Now get a grip, Josh." I pick up the broom from the corner and turn it on its end.

"What are you doing?" he whimpers.

"I'm just... testing." Tentatively, I poke the furry corpse lying on the rack. It doesn't move

"Aaaa!" groans Josh.

"Shut up!"

"How long has it been rotting in there? It'll be full of maggots. Oh God! Stop. Please, I'm begging you." I ignore him and poke it again.

"Leave it, La-La," he pleads. "We could get typhoid."

"Hang on... No... It doesn't have a face as far as I can see."

"It's been eaten away." He lets out a long-winded moan.

I'm just about to try and tease it over onto its side when the sound of footsteps can be heard coming down the hall. Josh lets out a gasp. "It's His Lordship Flay." I slam the oven door shut and we both shoot over to the sink, pretending to be occupied. "We can't both be here," I whisper.

"I'm not moving," he hisses, gripping the edge of the sink as if his life depended on it. "I need to be where there is water and I can clean myself."

I turn and smile at His Lordship as he walks in. A slight lift of an overgrown, tufty eyebrow is his only acknowledgement as he heads determinedly towards the cooker. What is he doing? Why's he going there? I can feel myself brace as he opens the oven door and watch in horror as he reaches inside and grabs hold of the dead thing. I let out an involuntary gasp, which has the effect of triggering Josh who shrieks again and spins round. Flay stops dead like a sleepwalker jolted into consciousness and lifts his heavily lidded eyes to meet our shocked gaze. He stares back at us as if we are strange mutants from another class dimension who have somehow dropped into his domain by some weird trick of circumstance. We stand frozen to the spot, trying not to stare at the thing in his hand – which, of course, we do – our eyes drawn ineluctably to it. Then, almost imperceptibly, a flicker of comprehension lights up his face and he raises his arm and waves the 'beast with no face' in the air. "I put it in there to dry," he mumbles, then turns and leaves.

We stand speechless, watching his retreating figure disappear into the gloom. Josh who, for some reason, is standing with his hands round his throat breaks the silence, "We have to leave, La-La. We have to go now."

I shake my head. "No, we can't do that."

"But La-La, they're mad. Seriously. We cannot stay here. Something really weird will happen, I know it."

"I thought it already had," I quip.

"Exactly, and that's just for starters. Wait until they really get going."

"Don't be ridiculous. They're just a bit eccentric... and... horrible, that's all. Look, I've bought all this food and I need to get paid, so we have to get on with it." Josh stares at the floor. "See, you're not itching anymore," I say brightly. "You'll be fine."

"Oh no, don't remind me!" His hand flies up to scratch again.

"Well, there you are, I'm right - it's psychosomatic. Just keep your mind on what you are doing and you won't itch. O.K?" He looks at me like an abused dog. "Josh, for goodness sake. I'm running out of patience here. Come on."

"Ok," he agrees reluctantly. "But don't ask me to clean the cooker or go near it and any more freaky stuff like that and I'm out outta here, you understand?"

"Yes. Fine. I'll be right behind you. Now why don't you start by trying to make curls out of the margarine and I will try and get some of the grime off the cooker."

I have to make a concerted effort not to gag in front of him as I scrub away at the filth and dispose of the cockroach carcass I find squashed between the rubber trim and the oven door. I know, in spite of our agreement, he is in danger of bolting at the slightest upset. Thankfully, our industry takes over and by some miracle, all is ready by the time the guests come to sit down. The sound of the bell makes us both jump. "The moment has arrived," I say jokingly. Josh looks as if he's going off to his own execution and crosses himself before picking up the tray of starters. I smile and wave him goodbye - borrowing from my mother's final farewell, when dumping me at boarding school, I say cheerily. "Chin up, darling. You'll enjoy it once you get into it and, before you know what's what, you'll be back here again."

He pulls a face and sets off. And before I know it, he is back again, hyperventilating and flapping his napkin. "It's there. It's in there!"

"What is?" I ask, trying to pull the meat out of the oven without burning myself.

"The thing. The dead thing. The thing without a face from the oven!"

"What?" I stop in my tracks.

"It's on his head!" Josh looks at me with horror. "His head!" He stuffs his fist into his mouth to stop himself from screaming then immediately pulls it out and wails. "It's his toupee!" The thought of the grizzly old toupee laced with cockroach shit sitting atop his bald pate after being in the filthy oven stops me in my tracks, but not for long, as another increasingly stronger sensation of scorching flesh overwhelms me. I recognise the oven cloth has begun to fail.

"Fuck! Ow! Ow! Fuck! Ow!" I mutter, looking frantically round for somewhere to dump the tin as the large leg of lamb slides back and forth.

"I can't do this." Josh shakes his head. "I swear I'm gonna start gagging every time I look at him. Sorry La-La, but it's too much. I have to go." He makes a dash for the basement door and opens it.

"No! Stop, Josh! Ow! Fuck Ow! Stop! Josh!" I call out in desperation, trying frantically to find a place for the burning tin, but all the surfaces are covered and he's halfway out the door. The pain is now so intense I can almost feel my skin bubbling up with third-degree blisters. I can't hold on any longer and with a cry, I drop the thing. It spatters oil everywhere as it jumps out of the tin as I rush to stop Josh before he disappears. I just manage to grab hold of his belt as he runs up the basement steps and I hang onto him like a bull terrier with locked jaws.

"No La-La, let me go!" he cries, struggling against my grip.

"You can't do this to me. You're supposed to be my friend. Friends don't dump one another like this. You... you bastard, Josh!"

"You know I'm O.C.D. You know that. This is way above my tolerance level." He continues struggling up the stairs, but it's in slow motion now as he strains to drag the full weight of my body behind him as I cling on. "Give it up La-La! Give it up," he pleads.

"No!" I grunt as I pull back on him with all my strength. "You are not going to do this to me. I won't let you."

"You're going to ruin my belt if you don't let go," he warns. "It's a present from my mom and she'll be very upset."

"Fuck your 'mom' and fuck your belt. If she knew what a shit you are, she'd give you a bloody good flogging with it." I pull down on it harder.

"Excuse me."

A strange, sonorous voice floats up the stairway and cuts across our struggle. "Excuse me," it repeats itself. We both stop in mid-flow, then turn to look behind us. There is the lugubrious face of His Lordship aka 'Flay' staring up at us, though he is a different-looking Flay now, with 'hair'.

"I was wondering if we could possibly have a jug of water on the table, if it's not too much trouble."

The pair of us shocked into silence are momentarily transfixed. "Yes, certainly Sir, I mean, Your Lordship. Erm. Yes," Josh replies, shaking himself loose from my grasp and stepping over me, making his way back into the kitchen, following the angular figure of His Lordship. I pull myself up and race after them with a sense of dread, knowing the meat is on the floor and the room splattered in grease and meat juices. I watch in amazement as 'Flay', ignoring the mess that is his dinner, lying forlornly on the lino, steps over it and carries on back to the dining room. I pick up the meat, wash it under the tap and fling it back in the oven. I'm past caring now.

Somehow, we struggle through the rest of the evening in silence until finally, it's coffee time and the end is in sight. The bell rings insistently. "Ok. Ok, I'm coming, you pink pig," mutters Josh under his breath and lets out a sigh. "God, I'm exhausted."

I load him up with petit fours, coffee pot and cups and saucers. "I'll bring the milk and backup coffee and wait out of sight," I say, affecting a conciliatory tone, as this is our first attempt at communication since the battle on the stairs.

"Ok. Thanks," he replies and allows himself a little smile. "This has to be the freakiest dinner party I have ever done in my life."

"You can say that again."

"If you've ruined my belt, I'll never forgive you," he says, adopting a petulant pout.

"Shut up you fuckwit and get your sorry arse back out there."

We are friends again - until the next time he tries to duck out on me that is.

"Which one's the ambassador of Uruguay?" I whisper.

"The one with the full head of real hair and the large nose," Josh replies, grabbing more cups and moving off. I peer through the crack in the doorjamb.

Madame Fu Man Chu watches Josh with a gimlet eye, pointing with one of her blood-red painted claws where he should put the things. Her husband is listening to another grey man talking to him and there are two women of indeterminate age over 50 with an empty chair on either side of them. I try to turn my face so it's skewed as far as it can be without my nose meeting the same fate as the cockroach in the oven door. I manage to catch sight of what I assume must be the Ambassador's back, identified by his thick hair touching the rim of his collar. He is talking to someone who is blocked from my view. Then he shifts his weight onto one hip as he settles into listening mode and I freeze. The person in the gloom of that dark room, talking back at him, almost melting into the fabric of the heavy, dark green drapes is instantly recognisable - printed as he is, on every cell in my body. Duncan! It's like an electric shock. I jerk backwards and knock into the service table sending the spare coffee pot and milk jug crashing to the floor. I run into the kitchen and stand in the middle of it, turning this way and that as panic overwhelms me. 'Get out. Get out now!' I tell myself.

"La-La, what happened?" Josh is looking at me, holding the broken coffee pot.

I stare at him unknowingly. "La-La, what is it? Did you hurt yourself?" I feel his hand on my arm steadying me and it's only then that I realise that I am hopping from one foot to another like one of those poor shell-shocked buggers from the First World War. 'How long have I been doing that?' I wonder in dismay.

"La-La! La-La – stop, you're beginning to freak me out."

"Oh. I… er… yeah. I smacked my head on the service table. I was just erm… looking under it for a teaspoon I dropped... er... Ow... yeah." I rub the back of it convincingly.

"You ok now?"

I manage a fake smile. "Fine."

"Sure? You should sit down for a minute, honey, you don't look so good."

"No. I'm fine. But we need to clear up the mess now or she'll use any damage to dock the bill. I know her sort."

"You're telling me She made me count the mint imperials before I put them out. Tight as a du-"

"Don't offer them any more of anything," I interrupt. "We need to get out of here as soon as we can." There's a beat as he looks at me disconcertedly.

"Ok. I'll start clearing away." I move to the sink to avoid his gaze as I fill a bowl with soapy water then follow him back out, holding the bowl with trembling hands. The bell rings. "Here we go again," he says, rolling his eyes. "Don't you worry about the coffee pot. I'll tell her you fell over the rug and say it's a death trap. That'll shut her up. Injury at work and all that." He winks at me and sails off confidently imbued with self-righteous grievance, albeit false. I edge nervously towards the crack in the door and put my eye to it. The format has changed. The women are gathered around the hostess who leans back in the chair as Josh bends down to give her the news. The ambassador is with Lord Flay and the other two men. Wait a minute. Now there's only the one. Where is the other? Where is he? My eye flicks round the room searching into the dark corners for his figure blending into the shadows, but there is no sign of him.

"Must have gone to the loo," I say, trying to reassure myself. I see Josh making his way back and, dropping to my knees, I start to scrub at the large coffee stain which has splashed onto the wall and the rug. My heart is still pumping but the shaking is under control.

"That did the trick." Josh sounds triumphant as he arrives back. "Pretty in Pink got the message loud and clear, said she would be out in a minute to give you the cheque."

"Where's the other man, Josh?"

"What other man?"

"You know. He was talking to the Ambassador. Dark hair, dark...?"

"I dunno who you mean." He looks perplexed.

"Yes, you do. There's Flay and then there's the ambassador, another man and another one." I count them out on my fingers.

"Oh him. He left."

"Where did he go?"

Josh gives a snort. "I dunno. I didn't ask. He let himself out. Doubt if he was making it to the 'Ministry of Sound' if you know what I'm saying."

"Oh."

"Why the interest anyway? Do you know him?"

"No, do you?" I reply sharply.

"Jeez La-La, why would I?"

"I don't know but you got us this gig didn't you? It was through a friend of yours, wasn't it?"

"Yeah, it was, but how would I have known who was coming to the dinner?" His eyes scan my face.

"Who is your friend? I mean, how does he know these people?"

"He's not a friend friend, he's just someone I met at Liam's place one night. What is this?" He eyes me suspiciously. "What's going on?"

I shake my head. "Nothing. Just... curious that's all."

"Yeah? Are you sure you shouldn't go to A&E? You might have delayed concussion or something?"

"No, no, I'm ok." I turn away and busy myself stacking the cups and side plates. A sense of relief floods my body and I feel the tension drain away as my shoulders return to base.

"To be honest, if I had had an inkling of what these monsters were going to be like, we would neither of us been within a tiptoe of this hideous mausoleum, make no mistake. There were moments during that service when I almost longed for my hometown of Winnipeg. That's how bad it was."

"I'm sure Winnipeg is nicer than you make out."

"Nice. Exactly. That is precisely why I'm living here. I don't want nice."

"Ah, dere you are." Lady Flay Man Chu appears in the doorway, her dress spotted with stains, as if someone had sent greased skipping stones skimming over the ridges of her spare tyres. "I have your money for you." She digs into a small evening purse and produces a cheque. "You leave now, please. My maid will clear up in de morning. I call you if I need you again."

"Not in my lifetime," I murmur as she disappears into the gloom.

"I can't believe the old Lord never told her about the meat on the floor?" muses Josh as we jam all the kitchen equipment into boxes.

"I expect he's used to his food being marinated in filth. I reckon the vermin here should be given free counselling for having to live under these conditions."

"Yeah well, I'm going to soak in a tub of bleach when I get back." He picks up a box. "Right. I'm going to start loading the car, honey. Don't you do anything ok? I've stacked it all at the bottom and I'm going to do it."

"Ok. Thanks." I watch him disappear up the basement steps and grab an unsavoury-looking cloth to finish off wiping down the surfaces. I glance over towards the hallway. 'One more look,' I hear my mind whisper, 'just to make absolutely sure.' I start to move then pull myself up short. With a sinking feeling in my stomach, the next thought wheedles its way through. 'This is the second time you have seen him. There can't be a mistake. He must still be alive. But how-'

"La-La!" I jump as Josh comes back into the room. "Is that all that's left?' He nods at the remaining two boxes on the side.

"Yeah, that's it."

"Let's hit the road then. Come on. We need to get outta here." He grabs the boxes and we head off up the basement steps.

The street is slick with wet in the light of the old street lamps as we settle ourselves into the cold of my 2CV. "I think a little spliff is in order eh? After what we've been through," says Josh, rummaging in his bag as I try to start up the engine. The car lurches as it struggles to catch.

"Oh no, don't start that," I sigh.

"Come on sweetie. Be a good car now," urges Josh as the car sounds like it's trying to throw up in its attempts to cough into life.

"I think it's damp. I don't want to flood it. I'll leave it for a moment and then try again."

"Ok. Got a light?" He looks at me, the spliff hanging out of his mouth.

"In my bag."

"Where's your bag?"

"I thought you picked it up?"

"No. I don't have it. Didn't you bring it out with you?"

"Shit! I must have left it down there." I jump out of the car and run down the steps. The door is still unlocked and I can see the bag squashed in by the side of the fridge where I left it. Picking it up, I notice the lights in the hallway have been switched off. I hurriedly step outside and pull the door too. Then something makes me hesitate. A smell so familiar and yet...

"I thoroughly enjoyed your meal tonight, Angela."

I spin round. In the darkness, a plume of grey cigar smoke curls across the body of a man watching in the shadows. He leans forward. A stripe of light thrown through the bars of the railings illuminates one side of his face. "Thank you so much," he whispers.

"Duncan? What... what do you want?" I see the crooked smile lift the corner of his mouth the way it always did when he knew he had you in his grip.

"Want?" he echoes. "Just to say thank you."

My breath is audible as it comes in jagged bursts. "You leave me alone. You keep away from me."

"Angela it-"

"No!" I hiss. "Go away." I bound up the steps two at a time. Wrenching open the car door, I throw the bag at Josh as I jump in and switch on the ignition, pressing hard down on the accelerator. "Come on you fucking thing, start for Christ's sake!"

"Whoa, steady girl," laughs Josh as he finds the lighter and lights up. The engine roars into life and I pull out and head down the road. The gears scream at maximum torque as we careen around the corner, the kitchen equipment crashing to one side. "Hey La-La, cool it, will ya?" remonstrates Josh, sliding into me. "I nearly burnt my freaking face off."

"Give me that." I grab the joint, drawing hard on it. After a few minutes, I feel myself beginning to calm and I slow down to a stately 30 miles an hour. I hold the spliff out to Josh who takes it gratefully.

"You know what? I think we should definitely go to the hospital. That bang on the head must have done something."

"No," I reply, switching on the cassette player. "It wasn't that. I just stubbed my toe coming out of the door. It really hurts. It's my toe, not my brain, ok? It's been a hard night."

"Toe damage. Yeah. Painful." He takes a drag and speaks in the strained voice people do whilst trying to hold the smoke in as long as possible for maximum effect. "You know why you're having all these accidents, don't you? 'Cos you're tired. That's why. We've been going for 2 weeks now without a break." He lets his breath out with a whoosh.

"You're right. It's all too much."

"I know I'm right, honey. We need to slow it down a bit."

"But I can't turn people down. You never know when the work will all dry up and I want to buy a horse."

What did I just say? Where did that come from?

"A horse?" he repeats. "Excuse me?"

I don't answer because my mind is whirling and diving and seeing images that I haven't seen for a long time; the liquid eyes, the flowing manes, powerful bodies, muscle lines, smell, strength, beauty.

The images of long ago. When they rescued me.

***

"A horse? Really, are you sure about that?" Jack looks unimpressed. "Why a horse? We have cats."

"Yes, I know, but I've always wanted one. Ever since Mum got a job teaching dyslexic kids reading, writing and riding. That's when horses came into my life."

"I didn't know your mum was a teacher?"

"No, well, she wasn't but she was a very good rider. She was groom to a top woman show jumper in Ireland when she was young. Anyway, it was when we ran away from Duncan and my dad disappeared. We were homeless. Mum saw the advert in the local paper and got the job, probably because she was so cheap, plus half her salary was in exchange for the tiny, damp prefab that came with it."

"No credentials and she was allowed to teach?"

"Yup. You didn't need it in those days in the private sector. Mr Anderson, the Head, was an ex-army chap who set up his own prep school. It was rather like the sort of school Kingsley Amis wrote about in 'Lucky Jim', except Mr Anderson was a bit more like Professor Brainstorm."

"Shame she couldn't carry on teaching."

"Yes. It was."

"Why didn't she?"

"The school folded. Went bankrupt."

"Oh. Couldn't she have trained?"

"No, Jack. She was trying to find a job with a roof over our heads and food on the table. Where was the money for that? No one helped her. No one helped us. When would she have trained? Honestly, you comfortable middle-class people have no fucking idea do you?"

"Sorry. I was only asking."

"I'm going to have a bath," I say and leave the room.

Chapter Twelve
THREE LITTLE PIGS AND SEVEN HORSES

Later on that evening, I climbed up into the loft and pulled out my old scrapbook and diary. Flicking through, I found the dates when we lived in the damp prefab. In it, I had written:

'I love it here with the ponies. We have only been here for three weeks and I have to go back to boarding school. In the hols, I'm going to help Mum look after the ponies and I'll get to ride every day. Can't wait. James doesn't like it much here. He says our house is like the Little Pigs' House. I helped Mum paint the walls. The house was full of old school desks and chairs and the walls were all grey and a bit mouldy. I don't care though because it's away from Duncan. It's our home. I washed the paint brushes and Mum put Kiffa (our dog) in the car out of the way as we were going down to the field to bring the ponies in. Kiffa's not used to them just yet and she wants to round them up. We opened the gate to the big field and Mum did a sort of pig call and the ponies all came flying up the track bucking and snorting and tossing their heads. They are very, very beautiful. Racing like that in a herd gets them all excited so they dance around the orchard going in and out of the trees before going into their stables. I love them. They are just magnificent. Having these horses makes up for almost everything. Can't wait for the Christmas holidays.'

Flipping the pages, I move to a darker place:

'Back at the house, we were just having a cup of tea before I had to go back to school. I was doing my usual thing of trying to convince Mum that I should be a day person. She says the only reason I have stayed on at the school is because she talked to the council and told them things were difficult and they said, if I did well with my O Levels, they will pay for me to stay on, but as we have no money, I must stay there so I get fed properly. In any case, it wouldn't be fair on James as he has to board at the grammar school for the same reason. Then suddenly, there was a bang on the door. Mum and I looked at each other. It was a loud bang, not a polite one, so we waited a moment. "Helen! Helen! Come out, I know you are there. What the bloody hell do you think you are doing?"

Oh God! My stepfather! He'd found us!

Mum and I shot up out of our seats and listened frozen to the spot. "What are you going to do?" I whispered. She shook her head. He started banging on the front door again. James was right. This was the Three Little Pigs' house and much more of that sort of violence and the whole thing would collapse. It suddenly occurred to me that he might come round the back and our living room had a big window so he'd see us straight away. "Quick, quick, hide in the bathroom." We scurried in and shut the door. There was just enough room for Mum to sit on the edge of the bath and me on the lavatory. We both looked up at the small window at the top. "He won't get up there," I said and we sat and waited. It was really frightening. I was right, he was circling the house. I could hear him trying the windows, then he was back at the front door.

"Come out here now Helen or I'll break the door down. I mean it." He really was the Big, Bad Wolf!

"I better go." Mum stood up.

"No, No." I pulled her back so she practically fell into the bath, which sort of made me laugh, though it wasn't funny. "I'll go, you stay here."

"No. I must go." I couldn't let her. She was really frightened and I knew why. So far, he had never hit me. I could feel a sort of fury rising up inside me, shoving all my fear out of the way. When I felt like this, it made me think I could do anything. I left Mum in the bathroom and made sure she slid the bolt and I went and opened the front door. My stepfather stood there, looking a bit surprised.

"Tell your mother to come out here," he commanded in his usual 'do this, do that' way.

"Mummy isn't here and I want you to go away," I replied and stared him straight in the eyes.

"Don't be silly, Angela, I know she's in there so go and get her."

"Mummy is not here and I want you to go away and leave us alone. We don't live with you anymore."

"Just do as I say, Angela." He moved towards me.

"Go away," I said, holding my ground, but my tummy was turning over. "We don't live with you anymore and we never will. Leave us alone."

He stared at me and I wondered what he was going to do. I could feel myself shaking but I thought I would punch him in the face if I had to. He went on staring at me. "You stupid child." I didn't say anything. I just stared back. Then he shouted out, "Helen, I'll be back."

He walked off and I watched him go to his car, get in, slam the door then roar off. I felt all wobbly and my heart was going nineteen to the dozen, but I also felt quite proud of myself. I vanquished the monster. Like Beowulf! I went back in and knocked on the bathroom door. "It's ok, Mum. It's me. He's gone." She came out looking worried. My poor little mum. She's much smaller than me. Only 5' 4'" and she has size 3 ½ feet. Weeny. She's so pretty with black wavy hair and blue eyes and a nice red mouth. She goes brown in the summer and has arched eyebrows. I have straight ones and Scottish skin like my dad i.e. white and freckly. I asked her if she thought he would come back but she didn't know. That's a real worry. Supposing I am not here to save her? Then, she remembered Boney and panicked, but there was no need as he was over at the school, playing with one of the teacher's boys.

Poor Kiffa was still in the car so I let her out and then, after another cup of tea, it was time for Mum to drive me back to school. Where we live is in the middle of the woods and you reach it down a long, bumpy, unmade-up road, so it is really hidden away. But guess what? We stopped off at the petrol station in town to buy some sweets for me to take back to school, plus a pack of 10-tipped Woodbine for Mum. The man was just passing the ciggies to Mum when, horror of horrors, a hand came crashing down on top of them. "Hello, Helen." My stepfather was standing there with a twisted smirk on his face. He must have hidden in the woods and followed us. We both stared at him, too shocked to do anything. "Yes," he said. "What sort of an idiot do you think I am?" We followed him outside whilst the petrol pump man watched us.

"Go and wait by the post office," Mum said.

"No."

"Go on Angela, I won't be long." I only went because she said she would be ok.

Apart from anything else, it was so embarrassing. My stepfather didn't care who he blew off in front of and I hated everyone staring and knowing he was a madman. I stood by the post office, keeping one eye on them. I could see them in the distance. He was standing over her and she was looking down at the ground.

Eventually, he went and she got in the car and picked me up. I asked her. “Where’s he gone? Is he coming back? What did he say? We aren’t going back to him, are we? Promise me we aren’t going back to him?”

“No. We aren’t going back to him.”

“Promise, Mummy,” I insisted because I had to. Mum still likes him, I can tell, but I just don’t know why. It’s completely crazy. How can you like someone who is so horrible to you? I just don’t get it.

I mean, once I saw him through the crack of the door to the drawing room and he was sitting on top of her and he’d got her head between his hands and was banging it on the floor. Boney was just a toddler, playing next to them with his toy telephone and obviously, it must have upset him as he started whimpering. My stepfather turned to him and said, as he kept bashing Mum’s head. “Look at Mummy, isn’t she funny?” I must have made a noise because he stopped suddenly and turned round. I stepped back ever so quietly and crept up to my room. I never told Mum what I’d seen. But I wish I’d been braver and gone in and told him to stop.

“Please Mum, go straight home,” I said when she dropped me back at school. "Don’t let him into the house.”

“Yes, Angela,” she said.

I thought, ‘she better not.’

I looked at the final entry:

Summer Holidays, July 27th.

'We left The Little House (the name we gave the prefab) for the very last time on Saturday morning. The weather was grey and overcast. Mum has got a job for the summer down in the New Forest in a caravan. The day before we left, I groomed all the horses one by one. I took their heads in my hands and looked really hard into their faces so my brain would record every little thing about them. I got some scissors and took a little bit of mane from each one and stuck it in my scrapbook with sellotape and put their names underneath so that I can touch them wherever I went and remember them. I don't know where I would have been without the horses. Nothing in my whole life can compare to them, although I really love our cats and our dog just as much, but horses carry you, you see. They take care of you. They shoulder your burden so to speak. They are so kind to do that - after all, they are a different species. Most of the time, people don't do that for their own species, do they? When I ride out in the woods, we meet deer and foxes and they don't run away because horses are vegetarians and they know that. In the early morning, it's wonderful. The spiders have spun their webs across clumps of wild honeysuckle and dog roses and the sun catches them and they glitter in the light. It's magical. It's just me and my horse seeing these things together. I can feel their muscles underneath me and stroke their neck and I don't have to say anything because we are so close and they just know. That's what horses are like, they just feel it. I think I'm a lot like them in that way.'

I opened the scrapbook, turning the pages and there were the little pieces of horse hair sellotaped in with the horses' names written underneath: Ace-High, Liza, Cindy, Delphi, Derwyn, Simba and Silver.

Their images, never forgotten, rose up in front of me. I knew then that nothing or nobody was going to get in my way of buying myself a horse. More than that, I would never, ever abandon it. It would be with me until the day he or she died.

Chapter Thirteen
TAKING CONTROL

It's Jack's birthday so I've pushed the boat out and I've hired a double-decker open-topped bus which I've decorated with bunting and a big 'Happy Birthday' sign strung across the front. The weather is perfect - a summer's day already setting up to be a scorcher.

As the bus draws up beneath our flat windows, I don my conical-shaped party hat with tassel and, grabbing the megaphone, shout up, "Will Mr Jack Barden please come down immediately and take his place on the bus. Mr Barden, the bus is waiting. Hurry! Hurry! Hurry! Don't delay! The magical mystery tour is about to begin. Mr Barden, sir, please step up and take your seat on the bus!"

The window to our kitchen flies open and Jack leans out with an expression of amazed delight on his face. "What the...?"

I can't contain myself and start jumping up and down on the spot laughing and whooping. "Happy birthday, Jack! Happy Birthday! Come on, hurry up, we have to go."

"Go where?" he shouts back, shaking his head and laughing too.

"It's a surprise. Come on!"

I run down the stairs and open one of the bottles of champagne that I've stored on ice in a bin tucked into the luggage hold area by the stairs. Then I whizz down the front and pull back the sliding window to the driver. "Here," I hand him a tape of U2. "Whack this on the tape machine. And here." I stuff a smoked salmon and cream cheese bagel in his hand. "I'll bring you a drink in a minute. Just got to get Jack on board and then we can set off."

"Oh, ta very much," he says, not absolutely sure about the bagel which he inspects as if it's a strange fossil.

"How loud do you want the music?"

"Loud. Very loud."

"O.K. If you say so."

"I'll ring the bell once to go and twice to stop, ok?"

"Yeah, that's fine," he nods. "Not being cheeky or nothin', but you haven't got a bacon sarni by any chance?"

"No, sorry. Go on, try it. You'll like it." He looks unconvinced.

I pick up my megaphone again and swing out from the platform, hanging on to the pole. "Mr Barden, you have 2 minutes left. This bus leaves in 2 minutes. Do not delay. Hurry! Hurry! Hurry!" The front door opens and Jack appears. "Hurrah!" I shout. He runs down the steps and jumps onto the bus.

"This is fantastic," he exclaims and picks me up and kisses me hard on the lips. "How did you keep this to yourself?"

Without thinking, I reply, "Oh, I'm very good at keeping secrets, didn't you know? Champagne, sir? There's bagels and birthday cake too. And you'll find a party hat on your seat!"

"Amazing!" he laughs. "Can I pull the bell?"

"Absolutely! You are now THE conductor of the 'Jack Barden private bus'!"

Dingaling. The bus lurches forward as U2 blares out. Clutching our champagne, we scramble our way upstairs to stand at the front.

The mid-summer sun beats down on us as we trundle our way through the streets of London. The bus turns into Sloane Square and I can see, much to my intense delight and amazement, that my plans have worked out and, waiting for the mystery excursion, on the steps of the Royal Court, are our friends clutching bottles of champagne, looking puzzled and surprised at the same time. Jack and I wave and shout from the top of the bus like a pair of kids and run down to welcome them aboard. I am ecstatic. I cannot believe it has turned out so well and I silently revel in Jack's pleasure. For the last three months, things haven't been so good between us, or at least something has diminished and I am afraid it will disappear. So, this is part of the rescue plan. The other part, I haven't begun, but I am going to, I have promised myself that I am definitely going to. The whole issue with the Duncan sightings needs to be investigated.

****

It's a Georgian terrace house in Kensington, away from the busy high street. It's unexpected. I presumed the therapist would live in a less commercially affluent postcode– somewhere like Finchley Road possibly - in a slightly shambolic, slightly run-down academic's house where more attention was paid to the books than the décor. The door is opened by a woman in her mid-fifties with a comfortable, lived-in sort of face. "Angela?"

"Yes."

"I'm Maggie. Come on in." She smiles warmly and steps back to let me pass.

I'm shown into a light, bright room with tall, thin sash windows fringed by expensive swags of floor-length chintz curtains and a large Labrador dog. He gets up immediately and wags his way over, welcoming me in. It strikes me that dogs, when they don't shove their noses in your crotch, have such perfect manners.

“So, Angela, what made you think you wanted to see me?” The woman looks at me in a searching way as she settles into her armchair. That was her job as a therapist I suppose - to search, reveal, winkle things out. What was I going to tell her?

“Oh I just felt that maybe you might be able to help me as I am struggling to sleep right now, well for some while actually. And, I think maybe, erm, how do I say this... erm maybe things... erm yes that's it.”

“Ok.” She nods sympathetically, still watching me. "So let me tell you a little about how I work…”

I don't take much notice of what she's saying because it suddenly strikes me about the enormity of what I am doing. “How do you feel about that?” she asks, cutting across my internal dialogue.

“That's fine.” I pause. "I have to be honest, I am not looking forward to this.”

She smiles reassuringly. “You are not alone, believe me, but I presume you are taking this step because you may feel things aren't quite right in your life?”

"Yes. I sometimes get a bit angry and... erm... well… down."

“Ok. Is there anything else?"

“No. That's all,” I lie.

She picks up her diary. “So, let's fix a date for our first proper session shall we?”

I have no idea how much those weekly visits to Maggie will cost in terms of sheer visceral pain. The sessions leave me dazed and monosyllabic for hours after. Everything I speak about bleeds into my family, like beetroot does with other food. As the mists rolls back, the landscape of those early years reveals something akin to Mordor and I have never, in all that time, questioned it. It surprises me how ashamed I am of my world and how protective of its shame. Nevertheless, Maggie sits there, listening to the chaos and hopelessness of my family. Each week, more and more memories and tales spill out; things I thought hidden never to find again clambered out of their locked rooms and paraded themselves in front of her, and for each one there was a footnote attached - 'It wasn't my mother's fault'. It was never, ever her fault; the woman who had abandoned us again and again, torn us away from our father and then served us up to her second husband, the narcissistic monster. She remained in my eyes, blameless.

"You mentioned you used to steal. I'd like to look at that. I'm aware most kids do it at some time or another. When did this start for you?" asks Maggie.

"When I was four-ish."

"That early?" Maggie looks mildly surprised.

"Yes. James, my brother, was very keen on stealing and I went along with it and then, I just carried on doing it when I felt like it."

"Who were you stealing from at that age, Angela? Your mother?"

"No. The local sweet shop. We were latch-door kids; it was something to do waiting for Mum to come home – or not."

"Or not?" Maggie cocks her head on one side. "Where was she?"

"Dunno. I think she was having her affair with my stepfather whilst my dad was still in Malaya where we used to live. He had been shot. He was a paratrooper. A Major in the Army."

"Ah. So, what would happen if she didn't come home then?"

"Usually, the old ladies who ran the boarding school nearby would come and take us to stay the night in the school."

"How was that?"

"Bad. Very bad. There was this white kitten-" I stop myself.

"Can you tell me about that?"

I look at the floor and swallow. I think I am going to have to cut this session short. All this is getting out of control.

"Tell me about the school?" Maggie moves on.

I take a deep breath and look up. "I thought they would make us stay there again."

"Again?"

"The school was the one Mum left us in after our grandparents had put us in an orphanage. She took us there after my aunt took us out of the orphanage. We were allowed to play on the swings and she said, if we stayed the night, we could play on them again in the morning. James said no. He smelled a rat, but he was older at five and a half and wiser. He was right. She vanished. We didn't see her again until... until..."

.....How long will the teacher leave me here?

I hope she doesn't make me go on the big lavatory. I'm frightened of that. The seat's too big and I'll fall in and then they won't see me and pull the chain and I'll never see Mummy again and she will be cross with me. I think my mummy has got lost.

Footsteps.

The lady's coming and I haven't been.

“Come on now, Angela. Oh dear, still nothing. Well, it’s no good we must get you into class. Just don’t go putting your hand up in the middle to be excused as you’ve had plenty of time. That’s it, pull your pants up – no, leave the potty and come over here and wash your hands.”

She’s not cross today. I wonder what they are doing in class.

“Hurry up, take my hand.” Her hand is cold and dry. I wish she would slow down. I can’t keep up. I think I’m going to fall. “Angela, do keep up.” My feet are going so fast, they’re faster than me. My arm hurts where she’s pulling.

“I’m sorry Miss Masham, Angela is late today.” Everyone looks at me. They know why. I want to hide my face. The old Lady says. “Sit down next to your brother Angela and you can do colouring in.” I like colouring in. I like yellow and blue the best. My book is nearly all done.

I can swing very high on the swing. I can swing higher than the boy on the swing next to me. I can see right over the top of the fence. Whoosh! Whoosh! I can see the fir trees behind the fence. I can see… I can see... a face… Her face! She’s looking over the fence. Why is she looking over the fence? Why isn’t she coming in? I have to get off the swing. Jump! Running... running as fast as I can. “Mummy! Mummy!” Trying to scramble up the fence. “I’m here, Mummy. I’m here.”

“James, Mummy’s here. JAMES!” I shout. “Help me." I’m trying to scrabble up the fence. James pushes me up. My knees get scratched against the wood. I can just see over the top and… there’s no one there… It’s dark. The fir trees are quiet and nothing moves. Where is she hiding? My hands are hurting holding on. I’m slipping.

Slip… falling… Ow. It hurts. "She was there I saw her, I know I saw her."

"No, she wasn't. You're silly," James says and runs off.

"She was, she was."

No one ever listens to me. She was there. She saw me look at her on the swing. I'm not silly.

At night, the old lady tells me to sit still whilst she ties rags into my hair and I don't like it. I don't know why she does it. My hair is straight and yellow-coloured. It's horrid with the lumpy rags in it at night 'cos they stick into my head. She leaves me a biscuit and some milk on the chair by my bed, but I don't touch them. If I do they will never let me go.

I hope I can go in the potty tomorrow morning. I don't want to be late for class again.

I sleep in a bunk bed on the bottom. There are other girls in the room. I don't know them. My brother James goes somewhere else at night and I don't like that. I think he might go away like Mummy. That's what I'm doing - waiting for her to come back. She went away before. She left us with an old woman and a very tall old man who never smiled and they frightened me. They kept us in the kitchen garden. One evening, when they put us to bed, James locked us in the bedroom and threw away the key and they were very cross and they took us to another house with dirty children who were like monkeys climbing all over a broken-down car and they left us there. There were great big green bushes with big purple flowers.

One day, Mummy came to see us. She picked us up in a car. I felt safe. I could smell her smell again. She brought us here. She said we could play on the swings for as long as we liked if we stayed the night. So, we did and I haven't seen her again.

I used to live in a nice place that was warm all the time. It was near the jungle. My Amah was called Pektchu. James's Amah was called Kim. I liked Pektchu very much. She let me eat my mango in the bath. I liked it best when I was with her and the other servants. I sat on her lap and we ate hot rice. Sometimes, I saw my daddy when he wasn't in the jungle. We had cats. Siamese cats. I loved them. I had my own. I called him Bopey–Bopey-with-the-noddy-noddy-tail because he didn't have one. I don't know how we got here to this place. It isn't warm. Everything is brown and cold. I can't see the jungle. We never have hot rice for tea. If my Mummy comes back, we'll go back to the jungle...

"Angela? Do you want to carry on? Are you alright?" I come to, shaking myself out of the memory.

"Yes. Sorry. I was just thinking. Stealing. You want to know about the stealing. Ok. So, James and I would go into the sweet shop on our way home from school and, whilst James kept the woman in the shop busy, humming and ahhing over which halfpenny chew he was going to buy, I'd stick a large bar of Cadbury's Dairy Milk up my front, then drift nonchalantly over to the door and walk out. As soon as I was out of sight, I'd bolt down the road as fast as I could. Once James joined me, we'd guzzle it like a pair of frenzied bull terriers and then two-thirds of the way through, feel really sick so we'd regularly dump the remains in one of the gardens on our way home - which was our undoing."

"Why was that?"

"The stupid boy who lived there saw us and sneaked. Needless to say, I got the blame because that's the way it was with Mum and James. He only had to look at her and she did what he wanted. He was the chocolate pimp. He had engineered it all, yet I was the one frogmarched down to the shop to apologise. I remember the bell clanging as we went in. No sign of the shopkeeper so I thought my luck was in but Mum called out. 'Hello? Is there anybody there?' In the distance, we heard the shopkeeper Minotaur stir."

"Is that what you thought she was?"

"Sort of. You could hear the dreaded sound of her tartan woollen slippers shuffling towards us on the old brown lino. My mum said, "Good afternoon. My daughter has something to say to you."

"What did you say, Angela?"

"Nothing at first. I wanted the earth to swallow me up. She wasn't very nice. The woman, I mean, I was only little. She had those double-glazed national health specs, pinky plastic frames, a puckered little mouth and purple permed hair. I do remember thinking, 'why do old women with white hair dye it purple or pink?' It's odd 'cos in their everyday lives, they're really dull and drink endless cups of tea with squashed fly biscuits and never do anything wild, and then they go and dye their hair mad colours. No other mammal in the whole world has pink/purple hair."

"Well, some do."

"Yes, but I didn't know that then. Anyway, in the end, I mumbled that I was sorry I took the chocolate. I swear the woman pretended not to hear so I had to say it again loudly and other people had come into the shop. Then she had a real pop at me. The rest is blank. It's called trauma, isn't it?"

Maggie smiles. "Is that what you call it?"

"I call it getting found out. Anyway, I carried on stealing from shops right up until a couple of years ago.

At school, I stole from anyone, even people I knew, if I wanted money. I used to take my friends out to tea in the local town on our afternoon off and treat them to whatever they fancied - sometimes at their own expense.. 'Have what you like' I'd say, like I was this kind munificent benefactor. You have to admit, it was pretty funny." I can't help laughing. I don't think Maggie thinks it's funny. She is probably thinking, 'Whoa! This one is really fucked up.' But then she hasn't met my brother James. The chocolate was a very minor thing, a taster so to speak for what was to come. Within three years, we were hitting the big time, touting my nice granny's diamonds to the jewellers in Edinburgh.

"And the kitten, Angela? You mentioned a white kitten?"

I stand up. "I'm going to have to go now." I pull out my purse and hand her forty pounds. "I've got the right money this time."

"Thank you." Maggie gets up and shows me to the door. "See you next week."

I nod. I cannot wait to get out of there.

Chapter Fourteen
GET A HORSE GET A DIVORCE

"Can't we just have a lie in, get the papers and have breakfast down the road and just slob out today? Do you have to go and see the horse?"

I have done it. I have actually bought a beautiful horse and Jack is not impressed with my new passion. Can't blame him. He's a city boy and the countryside for him is a theme park like most city dwellers, only good for the occasional visit or holidays.

"Er… yes. I could go later." That isn't my plan but I can see compromise needs to be on the table or the situation could degenerate into a huge sulk which might end up requiring larger concessions on my behalf. 'Is this what relationships become?' I ask myself. This business of barter for time and attention. Barter wasn't something I ever thought of when we first met. I would have thrown everything aside just to be with him wherever: dull, dirty or cold, it didn't matter as every experience with him seemed enshrined in a warm golden light of belonging and tenderness. I still belonged, but it was a different kind of belonging and it was beginning to feel restrictive. These are not good thoughts, they are beginning to panic me. I really hope I can hold this relationship together because I, of all people, know that going it alone is pretty bloody hard, especially as a woman. My home and everything in it, including the cats, will have to be portioned up and… No, no, the thought is too grim. But if I am totally honest, I am already contemplating the problem of how I am going to have sex with Jack in 20 years' time. I mean, how do people keep on doing it together year after year? I mean HOW?

We've been together several years now and, if I'm honest, it's all getting a bit boring. Mind you, it doesn't help having to wear a 'Dutch cap'. This contraption has to be the top passion killer of all time. It takes hours of practice to get it anywhere near your fanny, never mind fitting 'snugly' as the nurse so sweetly put it. It has never fitted me snugly or otherwise - it simply rubs and irritates and that's after the bathroom and everything in it is covered in KY jelly as the device, slathered in the stuff for ease of application, shoots out of my hands, skidding over the bathroom floor and ricocheting off the bath panel. By the time the wretched thing is in place, all desire has vanished. If only I could take the pill like all my women friends who pop it with impunity, but for me, it's like ingesting poison. Not only does my body swell up like someone suffering from dropsy, but a rash of Everest-type spots claim my face and it makes me mega mad - not just Jabba the Hutt mad, but Virginia Woolf mad too. I vacillate between the two extremes. One day, I want to wrench people's heads off their shoulders for simply breathing and the next, I want to drown myself in a river with stones in my pocket. I often considered this a strange way to die. It surely must take an enormous amount of courage. I've thought about that a lot. When Virginia Woolf killed herself, it was March, so it would have been cold and I have often wondered if her body fought her mind to stay alive. After all, the body's prime directive as a living organism is to survive so how would you suppress the desire, as you feel yourself fighting for breath, not to take the stones out of your pocket? I'm sure people hanging themselves scrabble desperately at the noose but, when they are found swinging, their arms always hang limply by their sides. Worse still, they often poo their pants, which is deeply humiliating.

As it is, I doubt if the pill and my hormonal madness would lead me to drown myself or hear voices like poor Virginia did but by God, it turns me inside out so, by the time I come out of it, I am exhausted - as is Jack. Jabba madness is more than enough to cope with so it's Dutch cap, condom, or nothing.

The problem of Jack and dull sex; if I'm bored now, what am I going to be like in 20 years? I suppose I'll be so decrepit, I won't want it. But Jack, dear Jack. Kind, gentle, organised, sensible, often-inebriated-by-10 pm Jack. And, if I'm entirely honest, dominated-by-me Jack. I wish he was tougher. I wish, when I suggest something, he would say, 'No' and then come up with something else. I wish he didn't drink so much, sweat so much, snore and drink so much. I fear I have emasculated him. I've become like his nagging mother, questioning him about his intake of alcohol and time spent at the club. Let's face it, what mother wants to shag her son? Correction - what 'normal 'mother wants to shag her son, because I once heard of a woman who did because she was lonely! Words fail me...

Driving back from seeing my horse, I reach inside the glove department with my free hand, trying to locate the half-eaten chocolate bar I had shoved in there a couple of days ago. Intent as I am in my search, I barely register the knickers I pull out onto the front seat, along with tissues, wrappers and cassettes. It isn't until I gulp down the final piece of chocolate that I see them out of the corner of my eye. 'Odd. What were my pants doing in the car? When did I put them there?' I have 20 miles to go and, in that 20 miles, I start to unravel the mystery. By the time I start the downhill descent to Putney, I realise, at the main traffic lights, that the pants, size 10, white cotton, embroidery anglaise on the front panel, ALMOST my pants - are NOT. They must belong to an imposter and they have been left there for me to find. In that moment, the world, which has been so comfortable and assured, the one where I can bitch about life and take things for granted, suddenly evaporates and becomes hostile once more.

Jack is in the kitchen making coffee when I walk in and throw the evidence down on the worktop.

"Well, you know what they say: get a horse, get a divorce," I say, looking straight at him. "I should have listened to the girls at the stables."

****

Jack stands in the now empty sitting room, briefcase in both hands, looking out through the open French windows onto the roof terrace. It's hot. The summer has been one of the hottest on record.

How has this happened? Where did it start? Memories and moments of another time slide into focus. How had we swapped those for this? Jack turns and sees me watching him. He bends his head and moves past me.

"Too late for tears, Jack!"

"I'm just sad, that's all, Angela," he replies quietly as he looks back at me. The pain of loss shoots through me as that horrible sick feeling, which has become a staple of these last few months, tightens my gut. I hear him go down the stairs and out of the door for the last time.

The silence echoes around me.

A silence filled with the noise of loss.

I walk through what was our home, with its once attendant hopes and dreams, now a shell waiting for other inhabitants. 'Don't look back' has become my latest mantra, but it's hard not to right now when all this place holds for me is the past. I will do what I always do and have done in times of loss; I will encase it in a time bubble that will float into my consciousness and then get quickly batted away until the years pass and time diminishes its poignancy.

I sit down on the stairs. The title of the book 'By Grand Central Station I Sat Down and Wept' comes to mind. I fold forward, my head in my hands. What made me think that I was capable of holding onto this kind of happiness? I had no schooling in how to deal with the reality of a normal partnership and in the end, it seems the splintered relationship was too easily blown away by a pair of white cotton knickers.

The cats? What about our cats? Like our lovely pets from my childhood, they came to the end of their little lives. The end of them and their role in the years of my life was a door shutting; a time never to be lived again. The death of my last surviving one has amplified my loss. Putting her to sleep has been as bad if not worse than any of this horror. Helping her to die, fragile as she had become, was like killing a child, because pets remain like children until their end. They still more or less behave like kids even when they get old, reliant on you to look after them and protect them. It would never enter their small minds that you, the person they trusted all their life, would kill them. It feels like the most terrible act of betrayal despite all the very best reasons for doing it. I don't know what is causing me more pain, the loss of her or Jack.

The doorbell rings. For one stupid moment, I think, 'Maybe he…' I clatter down the stairs and pull open the door half-hoping, but of course, it's not him. Whoever it was has gone. I'm angry with myself for being so stupid. Back upstairs, I collect my things and let myself out. I don't look back. Once in the car, I put my foot down and take the road out of the city, never to return to live there again.

I hit open country en route to where I keep my horse and try to think positively about my decision but it's pretty impossible to think rationally about anything as my mind jumps from one thing to another.

Arriving at the market town, I book into a small hotel near the stables. Throwing my bags into a corner of the room, I lie down on the single bed to wait until dark, knowing by then the stables will be empty of human beings.

It's gone 10.30 by the time I park the car at the bottom of the lane and walk up the track to the yard. The sultry air smells earthy from the heat of the day. The moon glows a soft, pearlescent ivory against the blue-grey of a summer's night. I step into the darkness of the covered stable block. Pausing in the doorway, I listen to the sound of horses quietly eating their hay. Every now and then, one shifts on their straw, resting a hind leg. Silhouetted heads hang over their doors and turn toward me, ears pricked. Their gaze follows me as I walk to the far end where I keep my mare. Slipping back the bolt of the stable, I let myself in. "Hello, Purdie," I whisper as she turns to register me. I slip my arms around her neck and push my nose into her mane and inhale. The pain and confusion of the hateful day rises up then gradually dissipates as I hold onto her. Her smell, her strength, everything I associate with all that is good, rests with my horse. Untarnished by the complexity of my own species, my horse, like the others who came before her, will help staunch my loss.

Chapter Fifteen
GETTING OLD

I've been living in the large old-fashioned house a few miles away from where I keep my horse. Aggie, the woman who owns it with her businessman husband, is about 14 years older than me. At one time, she was a chorus girl, but now she does the odd day standing around in department stores, trying to convince people to buy kitchen knives. Aggie doesn't need to work as her hubby has plenty of dosh, but she wants to have her own pocket money.

I cannot imagine why women end up being chained to someone for lack of money in this day and age because, make no mistake, she is chained to him, just as my mother was until us kids took control and threatened to leave. For her keep, Aggie deals with a man whose fragile ego makes him petulant and demanding. He is a colossal, albeit kind, generous - hearted, bore; a cross between Colonel Blimp and Eeyore. I'm sure he could find a job curing people of their insomnia just by moaning them into unconsciousness. He wears canary yellow trousers on the weekend (sometimes salmon pink ones), eats copious amounts of pork pies with pickle, and spends a lot of time mowing the lawn and complaining about it. On a couple of occasions, Aggie has enlisted me to spy on him through the crack in the sitting room door as he flicks over to the TV's late-night dirty channels. "See," she whispers. "He wriggles when it gets exciting. Watch! Watch!" Crouching behind the door, we splutter with a mixture of amusement and disgust.

It's odd how women subordinate themselves to men like him, yet hold them in such low esteem. I suppose, if we see it in terms of women's disempowerment, it's like Clinton said, "It's the economy stoopid!" Women have had to rely on men for so long for their economic survival, this attitude has become ingrained. But hey, here I am quoting a man who jeopardised his position as the President of the United States, undermined the Democrats, wrecked his marriage into the bargain all for the momentary pleasure of a bit of cock sucking. "Yeah, it was the blow job, stoopid!"

"Darling. Remember me?" It's my aunt.

"Oh, hello Aunt Maddie!" I'm surprised. I have had no contact with my aunt for many years, ever since Mum had called her Hitler, at which point all communications had ceased. Not that I took sides. I just wasn't in the mix. Their relationship had steadily worsened since the death of Granny and didn't look like it was going to heal anytime soon. "Darling! How lovely I've found you!" she gushes. "Saw you on the telly in something frightful, so I contacted your agent. A little bird tells me you've moved down to our neck of the woods again. Now you are nearby, there is no excuse not to come and visit. Do say you will?"

"Er, yes, of course."

"Wonderful! It's very lonely without StJohn. You knew he died, didn't you? Maybe not - I didn't put it in the Telegraph, but I did lower the flag to half-mast so people could see it from the road and, as you know, I hate funerals, so I cremated him without fuss then put him under the old oak tree by the gates. With the dogs."

"Oh, I'm so sorry to hear that."

"Yes, well, that's life... or death rather. Anyway, I no longer have Colonel Scragg living above the garage either as he had to go into a home. You remember Hugo Scragg don't you, he comes and visits now twice a week. Well, I say visits, I go and collect him. Unfortunately, he's not quite right to say the least-"

"Not quite right ?' I interject.

"You know, constantly scrabbling around in the memory department and never finding what he's looking for, then coming up with some quite mad things, usually to do with the army. I don't know. All very weird. But one has to be kind. Now, when can you come? It's going to be a lovely day on Wednesday so you can have a swim in the pool. It's heated now."

How can I refuse? I know I will get a grilling from her about Mum but the swim in the pool is too enticing. "Yes, that would be lovely."

"Oh, that's marvellous. Say 2 o'clock?"

"Yes, fine. See you then." I put the phone down and wonder how she had got my address out of my agent. It doesn't matter because Aunt Maddie is the type of woman who can ferret anything out of others when she puts her mind to it.

When I arrive at her place, the temperature is a blissful 25 degrees and I'm hot. I find her and, to my dismay, Colonel Hugo Scragg, poolside. Maddie is lying out in her shorts, her bare, brown legs dangling over the edge of the swing seat, sipping some alcoholic beverage. At the age of 70, she still looks amazingly vibrant. The unfortunate Colonel Scragg is dressed in his suit, slumped in a chair in the full glare of the sun, four sheets to the wind, and melting.

"Darling! How wonderful to see you. Say hello to Hugo, give me a kiss then help yourself to a drink."

“Hello, Hugo.” Hugo opens a lizard eye and squints at me.

”Hello,” he grunts then slides back into his other world again. Despite the sun, his face is the colour of goat cheese. It looks like it might slip off his head at any moment, landing in a gloop in his lap. “Come on now, get yourself a drink,” Maddy urges.

“Actually, I think I’ll go straight in for a swim if you don’t mind. I’m boiling,” I reply.

“Ok. Help yourself to a towel, there are plenty in there.” She points to the small thatched cottage shed which also houses the booze.

Being in the water is wonderful. I always loved swimming, especially underwater with my eyes open, but my joy was going to be limited. “Sweetheart, come out now. I want to talk to you before I have to take Hugo home.” Of course, I should have known better, the swim was just a ploy to get me over there. Maddie pats the seat next to her as I emerge from the pool and grab a towel. “Get your drink and fill me up will you whilst you’re about it?” The word ‘drink’ acts like a cow prod on Scragg who opens his eyes and rasps out. “Yes, I will if you don’t mind. Make it a vodka and tonic.”

“No! No! No! Absolutely not,” responds Maddie. "Ignore him. He’s had more than enough.” I smile apologetically at Scragg who has used up his entire battery of energy with this demand and, in a blink, slips away again. “Christ! It’s been really hellish with Hugo. I can’t begin to tell you.”

But of course, she does. “I couldn’t keep Hugo in the garage any longer - you know the flat above the garage, I had to get him into a home, which I hated doing. No one wants to be in one of those, let’s face it. Even the most expensive have that awful underlying smell of wee wee. But you know, Hugo was already losing his marbles before StJohn died and I couldn't possibly cope on my own. I mean what with my hip and everything."

"Your hip? Can't you get a replacement?"

"Oh, I've had one already. No, no, it's my other one now. But anyway, regards Hugo; There was this ghastly scenario when he fell down the stairs in the flat. He must have staggered into every room in the place, daubing each one with blood, then went back upstairs and fell down them again, where he lay concussed blocking his front door."

"The poor man."

"Yes. StJohn said It was like the Texas Chainsaw Massacre in there - not that I've ever seen it, not my sort of thing - but St John had and he was the one who had to rescue him." I take a sip of my drink and think to myself, 'Fancy Uncle StJohn having to rescue the cuckoo who had insinuated himself into his nest and then be outlived by him! Oh! Cruel fate.'

"So, you see, he had to go." Maddie takes another slug of her drink.

"Yes. I see." I looked across at the bent-over lump in the chair. "Don't you think Hugo should be in the shade, Aunt Maddie?"

"Yes of course he should, but I can't move him. He's a bugger you know. Won't do as he's told and insisted on sitting there. He'll be going soon anyway so forget about him and tell me, Darling, what are you up to these days?"

"This and that. I do a bit of cooking, and some acting and I get by."

"Ah, and how is Helen, I mean your mother?" she asks with a contrived look of innocence.

“She's ok. She's moved into a council flat."

"Oh. How ghastly!"

"Better than being homeless and she couldn't keep on skivying in exchange for a home."

“No. I see that, but really, such a dreadful thing. Last time I tried to help her, she accused me of being a Nazi - no, not just a Nazi not even a gauleiter, but Adolf himself. Of course, StJohn was furious. So, we've had to part company. I couldn’t have StJohn being so upset.”

Mystifying isn’t it? The way women do that. Pretending they have some agency of power protecting their sensitive, fragile, male counterparts who in actual fact, they are hiding behind? The so-called sisterhood had passed her peers by, entrenched as they were in the old world order and Aunt Maddie, along with her age group, had nothing to do with feminism. I expect seeing Germaine Greer filming her butthole for the world to see may have alienated forever a lot of women born before 1950. Despite thinking the suffragettes were wonderful, the word ‘feminism’ to them was tantamount to blowing off with audible velocity during a moment of prayer at a funeral. It is perfectly normal that so many of them consider their own selves, along with their unfortunate daughters, substandard compared to their male counterparts. You only have to hear old recordings of Babs Cartland, Princess Di’s granny, to reel with horror, at her worse-than-low expectations and dislike she had of women, including her very own daughter.

“By the way, Aunt Maddie, I really am so sorry about Uncle StJohn.”

“Oh, I miss him dreadfully, but I’ve got his ashes in a small urn, which is surprising really when you consider how big he was. Six foot five and in the end, he can fit into an urn. Extraordinary. I now keep him in the drinks cupboard by his favourite whisky. Single malt."

"Oh… well, that's not a bad resting place I suppose."

"I talk to him all the time. Sometimes, if I'm a bit low, I get him out and put my hand in the urn and there are some larger bits in there which I can feel and somehow that brings me closer to him."

"Ah… gosh. Well, I am sorry I didn't see him before he went."

"Of course, that was down to your mother's behaviour causing the rift. See over there." Maddie points to a tree across the lawn. "I planted that especially for Helen by the lake. It's called a Judas tree."

"Oh," I say, taken back by the sheer spitefulness of it, when, as luck would have it, Hugo slips off his chair and land with an agonised yelp on the ground.

"Christ!" My aunt struggles to get up out of the swing seat. "Help him, darling, or he'll end up in the pool and I've just had it cleaned."

Bending over Hugo, I struggle to pull him up but, although he isn't a big man, he's a drunk one and it's like trying to heave up a bean bag full of rocks. "I'll hold the chair if you can get him in it," Maddie says. "I can't do more because of my blasted hip."

"Oof!" I puff as I feel my hold giving way. "He's far too heavy. I can't." With that, I let go and he slumps back down into a heap on the hot paving. "

Hugo! Hugo! Help, Angela. Come on now," orders Maddie.

"Hugo, please," I cajole. "Hold onto the chair and then you can pull yourself up."

"Is that the sea?" he says, looking at the pool.

"Don't be silly Hugo!" my aunt says impatiently. He skews his head round to look at her as if, through the fog of alcohol, he's heard the distant beating of an angel's wings. "Ah! My goddess." He smiles a blurry out-of-focus smile.

"Don't start that business again. Come on now, get up. Angela, get him up."

"I'm trying," I reply as I get behind him and put my shoulder to it to push him. Somehow, I manage to get him onto all fours like an old dog, his head lolling in the seat of the chair, his hands gripping the arms on either side, but it is as far as he is going to budge.

"Oh God, this is hopeless," sighs Maddie. "This is the last time Hugo can come here without help. I mean, Angela, what are we going to do?"

"Call the home?" I suggest, thinking, 'What's with the 'we' bit?' "Can't they come out and fetch him?"

"No, no, that won't do. I said I would manage."

"But now you can't-"

"No," she interrupts. "I'm sure we can. I've an idea. How about the wheelbarrow?"

"The wheelbarrow? Then what?" I ask.

"Well, if we can get him in the wheelbarrow, you can push him across the lawn to the car, then we can get him in the car and I can drive him back to the nursing home. They've got strong women like Polish pig stranglers there who can winch him out the other end." She sets off, not waiting for a reply.

I look at Hugo clinging onto the chair, arse in the air, and wonder how I am going to get him into a wheelbarrow if I can't get him into a chair. Every now and then, he moans, "My knees." I can't help feeling sorry for him. Decrepitude and a feeble mind can't be fun - for any of us, I remind myself as Maddie comes round the corner pushing the barrow.

"I think the best thing to do," she says, eyeing him up from different angles, "Is to shove it under his bottom and scoop him up from behind. Right, you take the barrow and I'll steady the chair so he doesn't shoot forward."

I lower the lip of the barrow under Hugo's bottom and gently push.

"What's that? Who's that?" Hugo lets go of the chair with one of his hands and feebly tries to swipe behind him. "Is that a dog? Is it? Get away you brute."

"No, Hugo it's not a dog. It's Angela. Stop doing that. We need to get you over to the car. Now come on."

"Is that you, my love?" he asks, his voice taking on a lovesick tone.

"No. I've already told you, it's Angela."

"Angela? Angela who? What? What's she doing up my backside? Not that damn nurse again. I don't need any more of that sort of business up there, do you hear me!"

"Oh for God's sake Hugo, stop it! Ok, Angela, get ready. I'm going to shove him in." With that, she pushes the chair as hard as she can so that Hugo lets go and rears up then falls back into the wheelbarrow with a thud, narrowly avoiding cracking his skull on the edge.

"Jesus," I say, as we look down at his crumpled form. "I hope he's ok."

"He'll be fine. He may not bounce like he used to, but he won't notice because he's so drunk! Now come on, darling, push!"

Christ, he's heavy. I can only stagger a few feet before pausing to make sure my back hasn't snapped in two. The sun beats down relentlessly as I heave Hugo's dead weight of a carcass across the lawn, head lolling, feet dangling, groaning intermittently as one or other got trapped under the wheel. My aunt, in spite of her hip problems, virtually skips along by my side. "Oh, isn't it awful really?" she giggles.

"For me? Yes," I pant.

"No, but being old is so horrid."

"Well, right now being middle-aged isn't exactly a party."

After circumnavigating the beech hedge and the parterre, we arrive at the car, which, to my horror, is a sporty-looking Jaguar. Thank God it has 4 doors because the only way I'm going get him in is either in the back or the boot and, if reported, the latter could have ended up as a jail sentence for the perpetrators. I am forced to use the same technique as Maddie had by the pool. Getting the barrow as close as possible to the open back door, I decant him with one almighty shove, which propels him headlong across the back seat, leaving a line of dribble and faint teeth marks in the cream-coloured leather upholstery. I lack the strength to shove him hard enough, so his legs still hang out one end. "That's no good." Maddie eyes him thoughtfully. "Right. Come with me." Going to the opposite side, she opens the other back door. "Get hold of his shoulders and drag him, Angela, drag him." Somehow, I manage to pull the groaning Hugo further along the backseat whilst Maddie folds in his stick-thin legs any-old-how, hoping they won't break. Finally, she slams the door shut. It reminds me of Andy Pandy, the puppet on kids' TV, who used to get crushed into the laundry box with Teddy and Looby-Lu at the end of each programme.

"Well done, darling," my aunt chirrups as she climbs in and starts the engine. "I must go as I'm not sure how long he'll last like that." With a roar of the accelerator as she holds down the clutch too long, releasing it suddenly so the car shoots forward, she speeds off down the drive with the bundle of limbs, once known as Colonel Hugo Scragg, possibly breathing his last. "See you," she calls, waving a tanned hand jingling with gold bracelets and bright red finger polish. "Phone me!"

Chapter Sixteen
DON'T WANT TO GO TO REHAB NO! NO! NO!

Mum has finally conceded defeat and got herself a council flat living with James. After the scene in the bath, there was another one in a telephone box where he slashed his wrists and collapsed, so there was no alternative really.

The flat is in a small hamlet in Hampshire. It's on the first floor of a 1960s block reached by a steep set of concrete steps. The landing at the top is open to the elements on both sides, acting like a wind tunnel. The flat itself is a regulation box with no central heating and stone floors covered in some kind of dark brown laminate. There is an open fire in the sitting room. My mother explained quite clearly to the housing people that she had a crumbling backbone but it obviously cut no ice and she's expected to lug bags of coal and logs up there. I expect they thought a woman of her background had no right to be using up a council flat in the first place and she ought to think herself lucky. The kitchen is so small, you can swing round from the sink to the cooker to the fridge without covering ground. Its one saving grace is the view. Being at the end of the estate, it looks out across fields to the South Downs. A large oak tree stands in the corner of the nearest pasture, its spreading branches sheltering the dairy cattle that gather under it. I'm not sure that James or Mum gazing wistfully out upon this bucolic beauty gain any solace from it, or maybe they use it to measure the meanness and damage of their lives against it. Beauty can be a sad thing - an unwittingly cruel thing.

Before James moved in full-time, Mum had managed to make the sitting room look lovely with her few precious things. Small vases and odd bone china cups full of wildflowers picked in the woods nearby had been placed around the room. It amazes me that any of her fragile belongings had survived the endless moves. How many times must she have rolled up one after another in some old newspaper, tucking them carefully into one more cardboard box, hoping against hope that this would be the last time?

"Mum! It's not so bad," I exclaim as I look about me. I am genuine in my enthusiasm.

"No, Angela, it's not. It's horrible and the man below is forever banging on the ceiling with the end of his broom."

"Why on earth does he do that?"

"Because he says I make too much noise."

"Doing what?"

"Just walking from one room to another. No insulation. If I had a proper carpet, it might help, but there's no soundproofing. Every morning, I hear him coughing up his phlegm. It's so repulsive, it goes on and on. When that's over, he puts his telly on full blast 'cos he is obviously deaf."

"Ah… Well, at least you have that wonderful view," I say cheerily, nodding at the window.

Her face softens. "Yes. It is lovely, isn't it?"

"You've made the place look fantastic, Mum. You're so clever - and I can get you a carpet. I can do that."

"Can you?" She looks at me hopefully.

"Yes. I'll sort it out."

"Actually, I'm not sure it's worth bothering. I don't intend to stay here for long."

"Of course it's worth bothering. You can always take it with you, but if it helps the situation now, then it is worth it, isn't it?"

"You're always so positive, darling." She looks at me as if it is some curious trait I had inherited from some eccentric ancestor.

"You have to be," I reply stoically. 'You have to 'pretend' to be, is what I should have said. Didn't she remember she had taught me that?

The next time I visit Mum, James has moved in and has decorated the flat in true drug addict style. Flowers no longer adorn the room. "As fast as I clear up, he makes a mess again," she complains.

"What do you expect, he's a druggy." I grab a discarded plastic bag and empty into it an overflowing ashtray. "Do you think he cares for one minute what this place looks like? He's only interested in the next fix." I notice the carpet I had supplied now has a big burn in it. "What's happened there?"

"Oh, that. That, erm… that happened when he fell asleep. He must have knocked over the table by mistake with the ashtray on it."

"You mean when he was off his face." I can feel myself beginning to simmer with anger.

"He was so tired. He hasn't been sleeping and he must have-"

"Oh please, Mum! Stop making excuses. You could have all gone up in smoke. Look." I turn to face her. "This can't go on. What are you going to do about it?" She turns away and stares out of the window. "Mum?"

She shakes her head. "You know I've tried. I did my best to get him to see the doctor again to get some help, but he just shouts at me and says I don't understand and then the next thing, he's crying and telling me he's sorry and he needs to do it and the whole thing just goes round and round in circles. He says he wants to get off it and he has all these plans and dreams about how he is going to make money and the next thing, he's begging me to give him cash. I don't know. If only..."

"If only what?"

"If only I didn't have to try to deal with every bloody awful thing on my own. Even Duncan would have been better than... than..." I watch her small hand pluck at a loosened thread on the armchair. Why did it always come back to this? Yearning for someone who, in spite of their cruelty and derision, was better to live with than without. It reminded me of the Polish woman I met who flagellated herself with stinging nettles in order to override the pain of arthritis. "I'm sorry Angela." She smiles an apologetic smile. "I know I shouldn't say things like that to you." But she always does and I can feel the familiar warning signs of a migraine gearing up in response.

That was the last time I saw her before we had our 'family' meeting. It was supposed to 'help sort things out.' Mum had persuaded Boney and I to try and talk 'sense' to James and get him to see he needed help. We agreed to a get-together at Boney's as it was considered neutral ground.

It was a late October day when I travelled down to the Sussex coast, a feeling of dread fermenting in the pit of my stomach. The wind came in fitful blasts, tearing the leaves from the trees as if in a rush to get on with winter now that summer was over. Boney's old fisherman's hut stood alone and isolated on wooden stilts at the edge of an inlet, looking out to sea. With scrub and marsh surrounding it, the hut, clothed in black clapperboard, had a forlorn appearance. A handful of small boats rocked from side to side on the water, their halyards tinkling in the wind, an eerie backdrop to the seagull's mournful mew. Even if the sun had been out, the place would still remain inherently. 'Jesus,' I thought to myself. 'This is like the opening of 'Great Expectations'.

I drew up and parked next to Boney's old banger. No sign of Mum's latest jalopy. Maybe James had persuaded her to pull out. I climbed the wooden stairs and knocked on the door. Boney opened it, dark-eyed, as if he'd been up all night dancing the faerie ring. In the background, Echo and the Bunnymen could be heard. "You look ravaged."

"Thanks. Do you want tea? Kettle's just boiled."

"Yes, please. Milk, no sugar."

"It's no milk, no sugar. Run out." He starts rummaging through a cupboard above the sink. "I've got some dried Coffee Mate stuff if you want that?"

"That'll do."

I check out the Kafkaesque interior. In the gloom, a small table took centre stage with a typewriter and sheets of paper scattered around. One armchair and a window seat is all there is in the way of other furniture. "This is cosy," I lie diplomatically.

"It's all I can afford. Got it cheap for the winter whilst I write my Opus."

"Ah. How's it going?"

"Slow," he replies, gathering up a bundle of papers and stuffing them under the window seat.

"Bit lonely out here isn't it? Do you see anyone?"

"Occasionally. My old landlady lives down the lane. She's a bit weird – into tarot and Ouija boards and stuff. I go and see her when I've run out of food. Anyway." He changes track. "What exactly are we supposed to be doing today?"

I shrug. "I don't know. Putting the screws on James, I suppose."

"Oh yeah, he's really going to listen to us," he snorts.

He is right.

James sits like a man at a court-martial, eyeing us with weary suspicion, as Boney and I ask him very politely if he would kindly get off heroin, stop living off Mum, get some help, or ship out. We all of us puff away on one fag after another, pretending everything was very grown up, very amicable and totally under control until - "Listen you two," James says, chewing the inside of his mouth in time-honoured fashion. "Something you need to get straight; heroin has been nothing but a friend to me."

"If that's a friend," I start. "Then who needs-"

"Yeah, yeah, yeah! Predictable," he sneers.

"Ok. Let's put it this way. It hasn't exactly been a friend to me or Mum or Boney has it?"

He laughs. He actually laughs. "Oh, Angela," like I was some silly little twerp that could never understand the complex issues of heroin; like someone as pedestrian and mediocre as myself could never comprehend. "Right. I can't see the point of this. I haven't got anything more to say and I've got to split now." He gets up. "Can we go, Ma?"

"Oh well, as long as you're done, that's ok, isn't it?" I spring up, blocking his way.

James considers me with disdain. "What's your problem, Angela? I just told you how I feel."

"So you did. Now let me tell you how I feel." I try to suppress my desire to scream at him like a harpy. "You show no respect for any of us, least of all Mum, but that doesn't stop you from living off her and screwing her for every penny she has. It's all about you and your pathetic habit."

"Angela, please don't do this," interrupts Mum.

"Oh, for God's sake, Mum, stop! Stop protecting him. He's bleeding you dry financially and emotionally."

"My relationship with my mother has bugger all to do with you."

"Oh, if only that were true," I reply. "Every week, she's on the phone to me worried sick about you and it's OUR mother in case you had forgotten. Boney and I are her other kids - even though you think we don't count."

"Cool it, Ange," says Boney. "Come on, there's nothing to be gained from this."

"Yes, there is. No one ever tells him where to get off. We all pussyfoot around him, feeling sorry for him but no one forced him to be an addict. No one put a gun to his head. He's chosen to do it without asking any of us, and you know what - we are all hostages to it now."

"It's got nothing to do with you. If you don't like it, fuck off. I told you before, I don't need you around." James pushes past me.

"Angela, please." Mum stands up. "Please, let's leave it now."

I ignore her and stride after James as he flings out the door and clatters down the stairs. "How childish is that! Just like so many stupid men I know. If you don't like it, then leave, that's always their answer to everything," I shout after him. "Maybe you could get your head round the alternative approach. If you don't like it, I will compromise, I will meet you halfway, I will consider you. Of course, in Mum's fucked up world, you men never consider anybody but yourselves. You're all the bloody same. You just do what you like and us stupid women just have to put up with it. Well, I'm not going to anymore."

"Angela! That's enough," Mum begs.

I rounded on her. "Is this what being the power behind the throne is, Mum? Is it? Used, abused and disregarded! Well, I'm fed up with it and actually, Mum, I am fed up with you expecting me to do the same." I stare at her, daring her to challenge me, but instead, she shakes her head and picks up her handbag. "I can see this wasn't a good idea. I'm sorry. I shouldn't have involved you."

"Mum," Boney puts his arm around her. "It's not your fault. But we can't help him. I think it might be an idea to get some professional support."

"She's already done that," I mutter.

"I better go. Thank you for trying anyway."

"I'll give you a call later Mum," says Boney, hugging her.

"Yes, fine," she replies and turns to go.

"I'm sorry Mum, but really you-"

"I know Angela," she interrupts. "You did your best."

Standing at the top of the steps, I watch her small, thin figure make its way back to the car against the desolate backdrop of the cold grey sky, her hair whipped this way and that by the wind. I can see the angry silhouette of James leaning back in the passenger seat as they pull away.

"That went well."

"What did you expect?" asks Boney.

"Something. Nothing," I reply flatly. But I feel James' rejection just as keenly as I had before; like cold steel slicing through my being and seeing Mum, smiling hopelessly at us, before she turned to trail after her son in the pay of the 'devil', made it even more excruciating. Because that is what it's like - heroin; the thing that takes you out of pain just long enough to lull you into safety, before it torments you again and whips you back into desperation. Heroin. Like my mother's former relationship with Duncan.

"She doesn't understand all that feminist stuff you know, Angela. Mind you, neither do I half the time."

"Well, there's a surprise," I interject.

"Don't start on me. She's too set in her ways and too tired to take on all that."

"It's not difficult," I reply. "It's not like having to learn Mandarin or something."

"Well, actually, I think it is for her."

"Come on. Mum isn't stupid."

"No, she isn't, but she comes from another era."

"I know all that," I sigh irritably.

"If she thinks that everything she has done in her life is a total failure, where will that leave her?"

"No longer ignorant with a chance to live her life in the way that women should do."

"You know what I mean."

Of course I do, but part of me still hopes she will stand up and join the fight, though actually in my heart, I know it is too late.

"She suddenly looks old," Boney slumps back into the armchair.

"No, she doesn't. She's just under pressure, that's all."

"It's more than that," he says, shaking his head sagely. "She's wearing out."

"Don't say that."

“It’s true. She’s worn out and who wouldn’t be after a bloody awful life like hers and now having to deal with a heroin addict who is bleeding her dry.”

“It’s not ‘A’ heroin addict. It’s her son. Our brother.” I'm upset by the way he distanced James, as if he had nothing to do with him.

“Exactly,” he replies. “And it’s taking its toll.”

Chapter Seventeen
SHAKE IT, SHAKE IT

"You don't like people touching you? Is that ALL people, Angela?" Maggie the therapist tilts her head to one side, like a bird.

"Erm… yes, erm. (Embarrassed laugh) Ha! Ha! I mean, I'm fine with a boyfriend, obviously. I mean all of them I was ok with. It's when, you know, you go for dinner at someone's house and there's a peck on the cheek hello or goodbye, sometimes God forbid a hug, I just… erm... I just dread it."

"Ah, I see. When did that start?"

"Not sure."

"Well, maybe we need to get on top of this. I think I have just the people who can help you with that. What do you think?"

What did I think? I think 'For fuck's sake, is there no end to the debt you have to pay when adults befoul your childhood? More diving into the swamp trying to see through the murk, trying not to drown.'

"Yes. I suppose so," I answer resignedly.

November. The weather is as bad as it gets. November, my least favourite month, despite Brussels sprouts arriving in the shops with the last of the chestnuts. The wind and rain push against me as I make my way to the Centre in Old Street for my first session of Bioenergetics. This is to be the cure for my aversion.

The smell of everything macrobiotic assails me as I step in through the doors and pass the café on the left. It seems odd that fermenting food, i.e. rotting, should be good for you. What does that say about our inner workings, I wonder?

With a reluctant heart, I climb the echoing steps to the second floor where the sessions are held. I study the notices on the wall outside. Under HEALTH AND FITNESS, some joker has typed out a list; 1. Suicide and Your Health, 2. Skate Your Way to Regularity, 3. The Joy of Hypochondria, 4. Creative Tooth Decay, followed by: SELF IMPROVEMENT COURSES where, in room 1B, you can: 1. Whine Your Way to Alienation, 2. Have Guilt Without Sex, 3. Overcome Peace of Mind 4. Mould Your Child's Behaviour Through Guilt and Fear. That last one will be why most of us are here I think and, taking a deep breath, I turn the handle and enter a room full of (I am quite sure) other fucked up humans all looking either terrified or shut down.

Yep, I'm right! An odd assortment. At the centre, two relaxed-looking therapists in relaxed-looking loose trainers and a relaxed, practised smile on their faces. They are a husband-and-wife team and naturally, one is American. They welcome me as if I am joining a corporate bonding event.

My broken colleagues, of which there are about 9, are of varying ages. The thought of my Tuesday evenings being spent with the suffocating misery of this lot fills me with horror. However, it's probably the incentive I need to get the problem sorted out pronto.

We gather in a circle and give our names. The main man talks about the Bioenergetic process and gives a practical demonstration of how, through breathing and focusing, you gain access to those places in your body where you have stored your anxiety and how it can be released. With this, he bends his knees slightly, tilts his pelvis forward and begins to shake from the pelvis down. Then, his wife joins in.

Then, 2 veterans of the class join in too.

Then, a woman lies down on the floor and, with knees raised, begins to shake as well. I watch with a kind of hypnotised repulsion. I am NOT doing that.

"Alright everyone, let's start by getting everyone lying on the floor and bringing their knees up." Obediently, we all lie down and they administer to us, smiling benignly, encouraging each one to find the release.

"Don't worry everyone, you won't achieve this immediately, this will take time. But we need you to practice at home every day and believe us, if you do, it will happen." I'm sure I never want it 'happening', but you know, in for a penny in for a - hold up – what's next on the agenda?

Worse.

Much worse!

I'm paired up with a young man in his 30s. We are sitting on the floor opposite one another. He has his eyes closed and one of his hands outstretched toward me. I eye it with horror. I am supposed to take it and explore its feel with my hands and talk about what I find. Oh, now come on. Really? I feel as if I'm going to be sick. I'm frantically trying to find an excuse to get out of doing this, but I can't think of one believable enough and very soon, he's going to wonder what's going on and open his eyes. Worse than this, he is going to have to do the same to me. The very idea makes me want to bolt for the door. I stare at his hand; it's beginning to dangle from muscle fatigue and, out of the corner of my eye, I catch sight of the woman practitioner heading my way. I steel myself and gingerly pick up his thumb with two fingers. "Erm… yes," I mutter. "A largish thumb... and erm… two joints on… err… or is that a knuckle? Is that a knuckle on a thumb or is that only for fingers? Right, erm..."

The woman kneels down beside me. "So Angela, do you see what you are doing?"

Fucking stupid question. "Yes. I am studying the thumb."

"Yes. But how?"

"How?"

"Very clinically. I see you are not holding the hand or supporting it."

"Yes. I know." I am getting irritated. I mean, what the hell was this about?

She looks at me in a knowing sort of way which irritates me further. "Just so long as you can see what you are doing."

"Yes. I can." Does this woman think I'm backward or what?

She smiles and nods. "That's ok then." She moves away. I swallow. I'm not sure I can stick this out if this is what it's going to be like each week. "Ok, everybody. Let's swap over."

The man opens his eyes and looks straight at me and smiles. I manage some kind of grimace in return and reluctantly close my eyes. I make my body brace itself as if I'm going to be hit by a truck and hold out my hand. Both his hands take mine. One supports as the other takes the tip of my little finger and then... No! This can't be happening. No! No, please! But I can feel it gathering itself up, pulling from each corner, gaining in strength; the rising tide, the unstoppable wave moving up my body. I can feel it crashing through all my defences – past the stomach, up into my chest, banging in my throat, choking, choking, and I can't hold it; it overwhelms me and the tears spill accompanied by dreadful, shuddering, silent sobs.

What is going on?

I feel someone rub my back and a tissue is pushed into my hand. The ignominy of it all. I've only been there for 45 minutes and this happens. I can't look up. I cannot bear to see the concerned gaze of others – their pity or whatever they've decided I deserve; this person who they don't know, sitting in front of them. I'd rather have had their undivided indifference. I wipe my eyes and rub my nose. Shame always makes me feel angry. The woman instructor looks almost triumphant. The man just looks - without any distinguishable agenda - and I really appreciate it.

Mercifully, the class is soon over without a group confessional. I grab my things and scuttle out the door. I step outside into the rain-shiny streets and climb into my car, the feeling of mortification wrapped round me. Was it that woman's intention to break me like that?

The evenings carry on throughout the winter months as I force myself to dive into what seem like the bowels of hell. My fellow 'fuck ups' suffer from a different array of horrors. The elderly woman who had lost one child through suicide and had another currently dying in hospital from anorexia; the middle-aged man who hates animals because his mother preferred her King Charles spaniel (yes, my sympathies lay with her); the man who held my hand who had ripped his internal muscles from overworking himself in the gym as punishment for losing his girlfriend; and the public school guy, my age, who suddenly went for me because I reminded him of his mother whom he loathed. Charming.

We punched cushions, did the shaking thing, and other hideous exercises with one another like imagining your parent saying goodbye to you, then turning and walking away as you look after their retreating backs. All sad, emotional recall stuff. Truly unpleasant.

By the end of the second term, I am done. I am so weary from it all, I would have been happier being a guinea pig for a bunch of student proctologists on the main stage at a packed London Palladium. I reckon, if I can't let people touch me after this, then I'll just have to grit my teeth and live with it.

I thank them for all their hard work and fill my now available Tuesday evenings with attending Narcotics Anonymous - on account of James. Oh! The joys of being a Shirley Conran superwoman in rocking London at the height of her superpowers, spending evenings in the company of other troubled, floundering human beings. But isn't all this horror going to change everything for the better? Isn't that why I embarked on this journey of self-discovery? Actually, why did I embark on this so-called journey? The unpleasantness of it had occluded the reason for doing it. Oh yes, of course. It was to help me to sleep, and to sort out -

"Your stepfather Angela. I wondered what you think is going on on that front. Any more sightings?"

I shake my head and look away. I'm back with Maggie for a final chat. I've had my last annual guilty trip to the Christmas windows at Selfridges. Maggie has suggested these stop and I know she is right, but it's like an addiction. The anticipation and then the experience is all-consuming. For the period of time, I'm there watching the fairy tale scenes with little clockwork figurines in the guise of Cinderella or Gerda from The Snow Queen, drawing me back into the world of the child, where animals talk to you, where dogs aren't sent into outer space to die, and it all turns out well in the end. It is euphoric. There is a place where good people live and care for the animals and nature, where all the bad people are vanquished and banished, where children are saved. I'm back to being a child on my own terms where ignorance and naivety are the key to happiness. When I finally drag myself away, the wrench is almost unbearable and, as the feeling starts to fade, the recognition that this sensation can only be had once a year and can never be felt in the remaining 364 days is so oppressive that the withdrawal plunges me into a band of misery that can last for days. So you see, Maggie is right, this has to stop. She says that the little girl, the one within, my child-self, has to be allowed to grow up. "The little girl inside you bounces for joy until the hand of the real world jerks her back into her hidey place, but she can't keep on doing that. The Christmas trips are preventing her from developing Angela, do you see?"

Yes, I saw, but the thing is, I don't want to lose her. Her world was my only real refuge. How bleak would it be without her? I recognise my image of her crouched behind the door in one of the rooms off the corridor of my mind, her face, turned to the wall, is not a happy one. I think she may be something like the small red figure in the film 'Don't Look Now,' whom the main characters believe is their drowned child come back to life. Only it's not. It's a murdering dwarf who has been going around, slicing people up, dressed in a red duffle coat. Jesus, I bloody hope she isn't like that. I must have looked crestfallen as Maggie asks kindly, "What scenes did Selfridges have this year?"

"Wind In The Willows," I enthuse. "They set Moley and Ratty in the Wild Wood where they have that enchanted, spiritual experience with the spirit of the woods." The memory makes me light up, but within seconds crash as I accept I have to leave their world behind. This makes me well up. I reach out for her lovely dog, who comes to me with a waffly noise and I put my face into his soft fur so she can't see me cry. I'm so sick of crying. I really, really am.

"It will be alright Angela. You won't lose who you are. I promise you," Maggie says gently. God, I hope she's wrong about that one. I would love to lose who I am. I'd like a clean slate where the curse of the family, which I'm beginning to think is no longer an idle notion of my mother's, can be eradicated. I have no interest in swimming against the tide until I'm drooling down my front. "Oh, really, I'm not worried," I lie, letting go of the dog and wiping my eyes on the back of my hand. "Also, I don't think it is such a good thing that your lovely dog is exposed to sad people like me on a daily basis."

"I am pretty sure he is ok, Angela. I know him. The thing is, Angela, when a child is bonded by a deep love for the parent, they will often sacrifice their own best interests in a vain attempt to ease the suffering of the parent. When a baby is small, it is imperative that the mother is happy because, if she is happy, then she won't leave. This desire to make the parent happy is one of the things we may carry on past those formative years when it is no longer necessary."

"Yes, well, my mum's not going to leave me now, is she? I mean I'm her only resource, so I'm not frightened of that."

"She will when she dies, Angela."

Ooh! That was harsh. Right below the belt. But I'm back up. "Yes, of course. I know that. I've been through that scenario several times and I have to accept it." Only the truth is my need to get my mother in a happier place is still on course and I am running out of time. Talking about death like that has the effect of ratcheting up the pressure. I screw up my face and squint at the floor. Ok, so the Christmas windows trips are out, but I can't give up on trying to save my mum. There has to be a way.

"And your stepfather?" Not this again.

"My stepfather?" I echo.

"Yes. I asked you earlier if you had seen him?"

"No."

She continues. "I wonder, do you talk to any other members of your family about him?"

"No."

"Do you think he is still alive, Angela?"

"Do you?"

Maggie gives it a beat. "Well, if he is, he must be getting on wouldn't you think?"

I realise all of a sudden, that Duncan hasn't been in my thoughts at all and yes, she's right, he must be oldish. It's been years now. At least… how many? I'm just about to turn 40 so -

"And your sleep? Has it improved?"

"It has. I am much better."

"Good."

"Because of my horse."

"Your horse. Yes." Maggie smiles and nods.

Chapter Eighteen
LOVE

"Don't you believe in love?" Mum asks warily. I look away.

Love.

"Love?" I reply flatly. "I don't know what that is anymore. I have no idea what people mean by that."

There is a pause, then she turns and steps out into the garden and I feel a mixture of intense anger quickly accompanied by the usual wave of guilt. I take a deep breath, watching her from the kitchen. Through the open door, I can see her standing in the garden, her small figure framed against the flowering pink mallow. Her head is bent and I realise with shock she is crying. She's only ever cried twice in our life in front of me: when Duncan forced her to have her teeth yanked out, no doubt due to expense, and on her birthday when we first ran away from him……

….I'd got an exiat from school for her birthday, which came 4 days after mine. She was going to be 47. Birthdays in our family were important because Mum had always made them important. I'd managed to save enough pocket money, without plundering other school friends' funds, to buy her a Vogue magazine and a frozen Victoria sponge cake from the Co-op. I knew the cake would have defrosted by the time I got off the bus and walked the half mile to the damp prefab we were living. I couldn't afford candles, so I had gone to the school art room and made numbers 4 and 7 out of cardboard. I had picked some blackberries from the hedgerows on the way as decoration. I set the gifts up on the old school table we had in our one communal room and made a pot of tea. I got Mum to close her eyes as I led her into the room. I made sure the cats, Kiffa our dog and Boney were in the room so we would all be there to celebrate (James was at school which couldn't be helped). "Ok, you can open them," I said.

"Oh darling, how lovely," she'd exclaimed.

"Oh! Hang on, I forgot." I ran out to her bedroom and got her distalgesic. "Your pills," I said, holding them out and then, something unexpected happened. Her smile crumpled and she sat down suddenly with her hands covering her face and started to cry. Boney and I looked on in horror. "Mum. Mum, what's the matter?" I knelt down beside her.

"Oh it's all so dreadful," she sobbed.

"What is?" I asked.

"Our situation. Everything. I - I don't know what we are going to do. There's not enough money. How we are going to survive?"

When the only person in the world you can rely on says something like that it's pretty worrying. I didn't know what to do either but Kiffa did and she was straight in there, pushing her nose into Mum's face and wagging her tail and so I did what she did and hugged Mum tight and said, "It's alright Mum, everything will be alright. I know it will. I can help. Don't worry. We've got each other, haven't we? And I made Duncan go away, didn't I?"

Thankfully, she started to pull herself together, which was a huge relief. She blew her nose and wiped away her tears with the back of her hand. "I'm sorry, darling. You've made such an effort."

"Do you like the magazine?" I so hoped she did.

"Yes, yes, of course I do. Very glamorous!" She smiled, which gave Boney the signal to climb onto her lap.

"Mummy." He was worried at her distress.

She gave him a squeeze and said, "Are you going to have some of Mummy's lovely cake Angela bought for me?" Immediately mollified, he looked greedily at the cake, as did Kiffa, and nodded his head. I cut into it and the cream splurged out of the sides with the jam.

"I'll pour shall I Mum?"

She nodded. "Yes, thank you, sweetheart."

On the bus back to school, I thought I was going to burst with sadness. The birthday treat had been ruined. Maybe I had got it wrong. Maybe the copy of Vogue made her realise that she would never have any of the beautiful clothes or holidays or visit the restaurants or go to the theatre ever again like the people in the glossy photos did. Maybe that was what really made her sad. I realised then how very important it was that I made a success of life, but also that it was time for me to take charge whenever I could because she no longer had her hand on the tiller.

The memory dissolves. Here I am, 15 years on, and I feel I have failed; my hand on the tiller has steered us the wrong way and I have a mutiny on my hands, once again we are heading for the rocks.

I join her in the garden. "Mum?"

She doesn't look up. "Yes."

"Are you ok?" I am holding onto my anger.

"I'm sorry Mum, but you wanted this cottage. I asked you again and again if this was going to be right for you and you insisted it was and now you say it's awful and wished you weren't here. I know it's very small but it's all I could afford a deposit on and I gave you all the money I had. I don't have any more."

Silence.

"You told me all your life, that if you could only have a place of your own you, would be happy. Not only that, you agreed it was supposed to be the one place James didn't come to and mess up, but he has and the mess he has made upstairs is… I mean, can't you understand why I am upset? Mum?"

"Yes, Angela, I hear you. I didn't know it was going to be so noisy. It's the awful village hall. Every other night, there is something going on and, every Saturday, they have those awful discos that last until midnight. I can't sleep or read. I can't get up and down stairs anymore. My back is so bad and I'm having to sleep on the makeshift bed which is terribly uncomfortable." She continued to look at the ground, her left hand plucking distractedly at the stem of the Mallow.

"And James?"

"Every time I leave James back in the council flat to come here to get some peace, something happens.'" She sighs. "Last time, he said he had no money for food, before that he said the electricity had been cut off, the bailiffs had been round, then he'd been picked up by the police so I had to-"

"Oh God, don't you see, he does that so you keep running back to him - giving him money for the drugs, trying to keep control."

She shakes her head hopelessly. "What can I do? I'm so tired. It's easier to let him come."

"So we never get to see you - Boney and I? James has taken over everything including your time. But this… I can't sell the cottage now. I mean, Mum, we can't sell it now without losing the bit of money I have put in it. We're in another recession. I've got no work apart from being a sous chef at £4.50 an hour before tax and that's without a lunch break, and out of that, I am paying towards this, my horse and the room I rent. This is just a nightmare. Sorry. I'm sorry. I don't mean to sound horrible." I feel myself cracking so I turn away and walk back into the kitchen.

That night, I lie in one of the two little bedrooms upstairs. The one that isn't littered with the detritus of James's madness where he had pulled things out, started tinkering with them and left them in a chaotic mess all over the floor. Downstairs, Mum camps in the lean-to.

The moonlight shines brightly through the thin curtains and illuminates the little jug of wildflowers Mum had placed on my bedside table. She'd put them there along with a favoured small leather-bound book by Evelyn Waugh, ironically titled, 'When the Going Was Good'. She had always done this when I came to stay. Always a little posy and a book. I realise she must have struggled up the stairs earlier in the day, in spite of knowing the punishment would be many hours of crucifying back pain.

I haven't seen her for over a year because of the problems with James. Her expression no longer retains the childlike quality it always had. It's drawn and her smile holds no feeling of joy. The year we had spent apart had wrung the life out of her with the ever-increasing demands of my brother; his lurching from stupefied torpor to incessant babble then heightened panic when the next search for heroin was due. At one point, he had rushed into her bedroom wielding a knife, blaming her for his failed life, screaming for the drug and forcing her out of bed to drive him to yet another shady dive to score. My mother. He did this to my gentle, artistic, hopelessly romantic mother! I burned with anger. Yet here I am letting her down too because I can't turn it around. I need money for that. Always money.

I climb out of bed and go to the window. Ducking under the curtains, I look out onto the garden visible in the mid-summer moonlight. It's a quintessentially English cottage garden with an old apple tree and traditional perennials growing in happy confusion around its edges. Gazing over the old dry-stone wall, past the orchard beyond, lies a field speckled with sheep which slopes up to the west side of the village church. Other fields encircle it like one of those neck supports, whilst the rest of the small town radiates out in a muddle of narrow streets. How safe and reassuring this pretty picture of England is. How is it that my mother can't find peace here? Why can't she just tell James to sod off?

All my life, I had believed my mother's unhappiness could simply be assuaged by a home of her own. I thought the pain of her life and then my pain would be over with this collection of bricks and mortar. Isn't that what she had told me? Wasn't that what we had strived for all my childhood? A home of one's own, never mind 'A Room Of One Own'. Finally, I had done it, given her what she wanted and it wasn't any good! I feel hot metal anger rise up inside me. Slamming the window shut, I go back into bed, muttering to myself that I've had enough, that I will leave tomorrow and she can just do what she bloody well likes because this is it, as far as I am concerned. I hunker down under the covers and, turning on my side, I catch sight of the little jug of flowers and I know instantly none of that is going to happen.

Chapter Nineteen
FAREWELL

"Angela? It's Boney. Listen… Mum's really ill. I'm at the hospital. She's got heart failure. You better get down here. I had to have James banned from the hospital. He gave her some pills."

Oh my God.

Boney sits slumped in a chair at the end of a long corridor, head dangling forward on his chest. I walk towards him through rectangles of light thrown from windows onto the dark brown polished floor. It's like an Edward Hopper painting. Hearing my footsteps, he pulls himself up.

"What happened?"

"She was brought in with heart failure. Then James gave her some pills. He-"

"What sort of pills?"

"I dunno. Something from his stash of uppers or downers - to help her with the pain he says. I don't know, but it seems it precipitated a heart attack."

"Are you saying he caused this?"

"I don't know. She had a turn before, remember? However..."

"No! No!" I shake my head. "Surely, he meant just to help her. Maybe he thought she was in pain. You know he thinks drugs are the answer to everything."

"Well, he's been banned from the hospital."

We walk through into the ward. Mum is propped up in bed, her eyes closed, her pallor wax-like, her breathing laboured; the life force slipping away. "Hello, Mum." I take her hand, frightened that touch might be too painful.

Her hand: small, square, practical with large veins running alongside the risen tendons. Hands that could paint and draw, that could create beautiful things, but had been condemned to a life of scrubbing, mending, washing, cooking - base domesticity.

She slowly opens her eyes. "Hello, darling," she whispers.

"I'm so sorry Mum, you've had such a ghastly time."

She smiles. "It's been a bit grim." The world my mother knew and understood, to which she ultimately belonged, was encapsulated in those words. The indoctrination of stoicism the war generation had been raised on was still there to serve her.

This was the girl who took her pet goat for long walks over the heath whilst daydreaming of being loved by kind parents; the girl who idolised her disinterested Victorian father who had no time for a daughter: the girl who invited another girl to stay for a weekend without telling either parents - hiding her under the grand piano, feeding her with food from her plate secreted in her napkin. The girl who got expelled from two Belgian convents when not allowed to come home for the holidays; who locked a nun in her room; who set out on a rowing boat in the grounds at night under the moonlight until she found the boat was sinking and had to be rescued; the girl who offered to hit other girls over the head with a hammer as a joke until one responded, "Oh for the love of God, I do Helen," so that she complied and she was once again expelled. Further on and now the woman who told the vicar at her niece's christening that it occurred to her she could not, in all conscience, reject the devil; the woman who hitchhiked from Hampshire all the way to the Highlands in Scotland and back to take a birthday present to her son in his far-away boarding school in an attempt to assuage his homesickness; the woman who's knickers fell down at the zoo when the old elastic gave way and told us to meet her at the polar bears; the woman who lasted 3 minutes on a bucking horse for a bet and ended up unconscious; the woman who taught me all animals are sentient beings and have a voice; the woman who worked as a nanny in Kenya, leaving for home just before the family were slaughtered by the Mau Mau and who met a man on a boat from Ireland opening his coat to reveal a pig he was smuggling. The woman who, desperate for love, gave herself to her first boyfriend only to be told he would never, ever marry someone who 'did that sort of thing'; the woman who then had to have a backstreet abortion and suffer the disgust of her parents; the woman who married my father to make up for the aborted child and who's second husband coerced, humiliated and assaulted her; the woman who lived in a time where women had no real rights. The woman who tried to make amends for the times she had abandoned her oldest children but could never tell us why or sorry. The woman who I loved with the visceral pain of a deep, open wound. The one who I wished I had never loved. This was my pretty, multi-talented, curious, loving, kind, fun, inventive, unlucky, weak, abused, abusive mother.

That I could not save.

"I'm so sorry Mum." I squeeze her hand. She closes her eyes. "I'm so sorry, it's all been... you know... the cottage and James... and everything. Everything... I know you did your best."

She opens her eyes and looks searchingly into mine. "Yes. I did my best." She half-gasps and I realise this is not a mere statement of fact or a simple testament to what she has endured, but an apology too. She closes her eyes again and reaches for the oxygen mask.

'The doctor wants to see us." Boney nods behind him to a youngish man with a nurse at his side.

"Ok. Be back in a minute, Mum." As I get up, I feel her hand pluck feebly at my arm. "What is it?" I bend down close to her.

"I don't... want... to die... in here. Get me out. Angela, get me out."

I nod. "Ok. Ok. Mum."

'"Angela." Boney is tugging at my sleeve.

"Coming." I follow him and the young doctor into a room where people are taken to be told the worst. I wonder if the walls of the place are so soaked in sadness that the bricks hold the desolation for years to come and haunt the people who have to work there.

I cry. Boney doesn't. The doctor leaves us.

"She doesn't want to die in here," I say, rubbing the tears into my mascara which makes my eyes stream even more.

"What?"

"She asked me to get her out."

"To go where?"

"I don't know. I'm in a rented room so she can't come to me."

"Nor me. You know the size of my place and it's in London which she hates and I'm off to Saudi next month to teach for a year and I've given notice."

"Maybe we could try and rent a place for a week?"

"Jesus Christ." Boney lets out a sigh and runs his hand through his hair. "With what? You're strapped for cash and I've got shit all, that's why I'm going to the hell hole Saudi, the last place on this earth I want to be."

"We'll have to put it on a credit card - I don't know -whatever - but I am not going to let her down now. Not now. You don't get another go at dying." Then I start choking up. "I'll find somewhere. I will."

"How about her niece, Nessa?" Boney interrupts. "She might help. Mum spent a lot of time with her - playing her piano and getting plastered. She and her get on well, don't they?" Boney looks up at me hopefully. "She rents a cottage in one of the Wallops in Wiltshire. It's tiny but it's right bang in the middle of the countryside down an unmade-up track. I went there with Mum a couple of years ago."

"Have you got her number?"

He shakes his head. "No. Sorry. But you know who does..."

"Aunt Maddie. Of course. Problem is Nessa hasn't spoken to her for 3 years after Maddie threatened to take her kids off her."

"Ah, that sorry tale." Boney shakes his head.

"Which means we'd have to tell Maddie Mum was dying in order to get Nessa's number and I don't want to do that until I have ok'd it with Mum. After all, they haven't spoken for many years since the Nazi incident. Supposing she doesn't want to see Maddie? You know what Maddie's like, she'll insist and push her way in regardless." I can imagine her storming her way through the ward with the heft and ballast of a dray horse, demanding loudly to know where her sister lay dying.

"Excuse me." The doctor puts his head round the door. "Sorry, but er... are you alright? I mean, I wonder if you are finished in here. It's just that..." He nods behind him to three people with strained expressions, waiting to hear their bad news.

"Yes. Thanks." Boney and I move to the door.

I manage after several phone calls, running up and downstairs to the public phone box, to get hold of Nessa who kindly agrees to have Mum. Then it takes a public standoff between the consultant and I to allow an ambulance to ferry my mother there. He says she isn't fit to travel but I know she will be relieved that she is getting out of the hospital and, once we settle in at Nessa's, she will relax. After the local doctor comes and administers morphine, I am right. Once installed in Nessa's own bed with a view of the hills and songbirds swinging off the bird feeder, her pained expression clears.

Nessa sleeps in the spare bedroom whilst Boney and I sleep on the floor somewhere. I can't remember where.

"Angela, hello. Sorry to bother you as I know your mother isn't well, but I need 100 parmesan biscuits and some petit brioche for a wedding on Saturday. I'll make it worth your while." Desperate for any money, I agree to do the job and pay Nessa for the electricity. During the 4 days it takes for our mother to let go of this world, I cook. Not such a bad thing. Keeps me occupied as my mind runs over and over things in a helpless way, as if in a maze, returning again and again to a dead end.

Aunt Maddie eventually gets the green light and comes up to say her goodbyes. I warn Mum she is coming. By this time, she can only respond with a knit of her brows but, in the end, she is leaving, never to see her again and what does it all matter? Dying means you never have to face anyone again so you might as well just let it go.

Lunchtime on the fourth day and, just as the Parmesan biscuits are baking, the MacMillan nurse comes down to say she thinks Mum is going.

At one o'clock on the Tuesday, Boney and I stand at the bottom of her bed and stare nonplussed at her lifeless body - the empty shell that had been our mother.

She dies in Wiltshire on February 11th. A bright, cold day. Snowdrops in the woods.

The biscuits burn to a cinder.

Chapter Twenty
IT HURTS TO BE ALIVE AND OBSOLETE

21st Century: 'To be, in other words, still a living woman, and to be told every day that you are not a woman but a tired object that should disappear. That you are not a person but a joke. I am bitter and frustrated and wasted, but don't you pretend that I am not as alive as you are and that I do not suffer from the category into which you are forcing me. It hurts to be alive and obsolete' - Zoe Loss

The time has come, as it does to most women, when I have become invisible, irrelevant and an insomniac. The menopause has closed in on me. Having prematurely celebrated the end of gut-wrenching monthlies, manic episodes accompanied by blood-soaked pants, the next stage my hormones were eager for me to experience is that which must not be named. As if the 2 years of endometriosis weren't enough, my body was duty-bound to show me the delights of turning into a human furnace at night and a zombie during the day. You wonder about global warming? Look no further than the millions of women sitting on doorsteps in the middle of a freezing cold night night, trying to prevent themselves from spontaneously combusting, whilst their temperatures hit the high mark warming the earth's atmosphere. It's a menace on a global scale.

Its other accompaniments include eczema, depression, allergies, loss of libido, osteoporosis, migraines, a tyre encircling the waist and the incapacity to remember words so that every conversation is based on the team game 'Give Us A Clue'. Turning 50 has been like metamorphosing into an entirely other being, as far as society seems to be concerned, and in this strange other state, I am finding it hard to navigate my way through a life that looks the same but really isn't. It has shrivelled. I have little work, hit by another recession which has somehow skewered me into owing a portion of £7 million (hello) with 5 others (no, don't ask) and prey to... Aunt Maddie.

I've been coerced into going with her to Vienna.

She is barely talking to me as we sit in the back of the taxi heading to Heathrow.

It transpires that I committed the heinous crime of failing to ring her exactly when I said I would. So I must be punished. Frosty silence hangs over us.

I wonder, as I look out of the window at the fleet of passing cars, how I'm going to survive 4 days at the beck and call of a woman who I now know to be an 'A-grade narcissist' with a borderline personality disorder, though borderline is being conservative. She is knee-deep. "I had a terrible evening with my dog Mungo yesterday David," Maddie says, ignoring me and addressing the taxi driver.

"Oh, how's that Mrs Jensen?"

"The fireworks David. They drive him mad. He was barking and barking. I thought it would never end."

"Oh, they don't like the noise, do they?"

"No, they don't. You can imagine David, I was kept awake for ages –some time around midnight and now I feel like a wrung-out piece of old string."

"I'm sorry to hear that Mrs Jensen. Let's hope your holiday will do you good."

"Well, let's hope. One lives in hope David." A sly flick of the eyes my way as she repeats his name as if they are old friends.

David makes the error of asking me if I've ever been to Vienna and by so doing, he shatters the apparently exclusive friendship my aunt has constructed, of which he is gloriously unaware. I respond cheerfully, "Yes David, I have once but briefly. How about you… David?"

"Don't distract David when he's driving," snaps Maddie and the rest of the journey is completed in silence.

I feel like I'm 7 again where grown-ups can bully you once more. With Maddie's lover Hugo now deceased and her husband StJohn long gone, she has need of fresh prey. Raw as I am after Mum's death and burgeoned with self-imposed guilt, I have been thinking I should try to emulate Jesus or surrender to my 'higher consciousness' by believing in the best of humanity. However, Maddie's narcissistic disorder, hidden from me in the past under the protection of her husband and lover has been revealing itself over the last months like the dance of the 7 veils. I'm frightened the final drop might not be too pleasant.

At first, I had been perplexed. My aunt had always appeared to me to be a fairly normal, eccentric, egotistical snob - perfectly common amongst people from our background. However, her daughter Nessa had alerted me to another more sinister side. One where she wore all black to her wedding and took out a bet at William Hills where her daughter's marriage wouldn't last for more than 2 years. "How much did she win?"

"Boney!" I admonished.

"Didn't say," replied Nessa. "Of course, I only married him to get away from her."

"Didn't StJohn say anything? I mean, what did he think?"

"Oh StJohn - the Ian Brady to her Myra Hindley!"

"Surely not!" I protested.

"Well not far off. StJohn had almost given up by this time. Don't forget he'd been in the firing line for years and he was tiring. After all, he's not my father - well not that I knew at the time, since she hadn't bothered to tell me."

Well hello! "Another story for another time." Nessa shook her head and downed the rest of her drink in one gulp.

"I do remember her telling me that at one of her famed parties, she did a headstand in front of everyone, forgetting that she hadn't any knickers on."

"She didn't forget," snorted Nessa.

"Really?" Boney grimaced.

"Any attention is good attention as far as she's concerned."

I suppose in hindsight I should have taken heed of the warning signs, but distress and guilt were making me adopt a different response to life. I was attempting to cultivate a softer, more tolerant attitude, one which might allow me to climb up out of that dark hole I had fallen into.

"Anyway, forget her. Anyone special in your life these days?" asked Nessa. "Anyone on the horizon?"

"No." I shook my head. I wasn't about to tell her of the three men who had come forward and offered themselves up as potential lovers during the interim years. These three became the first recipients of my new compassionate template, so I tried to accept their attention with grace. I mean, they were nice enough as friends but, as I explained to the first applying for the post, "I'm sorry, we have been friends so long, it would be like fucking my brother." I didn't add, "Besides, I don't find you remotely attractive."

The second suitor was harder to shake off as he was more determined; I might go so far as to say, wiley. He tried to manipulate me into surrendering to him under the guise of offering me help as a new age guru, instructing me in how to be in touch with my emotions in a positive way. "You know, Ange," he said as he sipped his ginger tea with added turmeric, chucking a selection of vitamin pills down his throat. "I've always felt like you are hiding."

'Behind a door,' I thought, thinking of that little girl in my head

"Hiding, y'know, behind a carapace of armour. If only you could trust and just let yourself surrender to the world, I know you would feel so much better." I nodded thoughtfully, avoiding his searching gaze. "Listen." He inched forward in his chair, looking deep into my eyes. "I do this amazing light touch therapy that I think you would really benefit from. Why don't you let me give you one?"

"G-Give me one?" My heart started to pump.

"Treatment."

"Oh!" I couldn't think of anything more distasteful, but here I was, on this new path of enlightenment, so maybe... maybe I should go for it. "Err, well, ok. Yes. That's kind."

"We could do it now before I go back to London." He eyed me expectantly. "I have my massage table in the car. I'll just go and get it whilst you change."

"Change?" I choked.

"Yes. Into something looser. Or maybe just a blanket or towel too so you don't get cold." He smiled, dare I say wolfishly, because at that moment, I knew exactly how Little Red Riding Hood must have felt, once upon a time.

As I made my way with reluctant tread upstairs to 'change,' I scrambled through all the avoidance strategies I could think of but realised, as I heard the click of the car door and footsteps on the gravel, accompanied by a grunt, as he lifted the massage table through the front door, there was no way out. No way out physically I told myself, but mentally I could block it. Yes. That was the answer. I went to the suitcase that held Mum's belongings which I had taken from Nessa when we left, which included Granny's (yes, the horrid granny's) flannel nightie that Mum had actually died in. I hadn't had the strength to let it go and it remained unwashed with her smell on it and some dried blood on the collar, where the tubes had been fed into her neck. I know it sounds ghoulish but who would have guessed it would have come in handy as a defence in my time of need? Wearing this would be the perfect antidote to any funny business he might be hoping for. The blood of my dead mother imbued with the spirit of my horrid, narcissistic grandmother was a perfect barrier. I would endure his therapy in the safe belief that he would be feeling their vibes and as such any hanky panky would not only be inappropriate but actually rather repellant. I put it on and looked in the mirror. I looked frightful. His startled look, as I came into the room confirmed it.

I never saw him again.

The third suitor was one of my choosing, albeit briefly. It was the result of an acting job up in Scotland where I had done that stupid thing, mostly silly young actresses do, which was to fall for the character an actor was playing, not the actor himself. Ridiculous, since I was no longer a silly young anything, but it offered me an escape, a diversion from the nihilism that engulfed me.

The actor in question had split up with his wife and had been living fast and loose. He was a pigeon fancier from the rougher part of Glasgow and his talent was seductive. After the play closed, he travelled down to stay overnight with me on two rather disappointing occasions. Unfortunately, it became evident that his character on stage was far more interesting than the man himself, pigeons or no, so I sent him a 'Dear John' letter and thought that would be the end of it.

Until, that is, a couple of weeks later. It was 1.30 in the morning when I was woken by Aggie stumbling into my room clutching the phone "It's for you," she mumbled, half asleep. "I think it's urgent." She tottered off back to bed. Immediately, a cold knot of fear gripped my stomach. James. What trouble was he in now? I hadn't heard from him for some time, despite a shaky period of reconciliation.

"Hello?"

"Is that Angela Fleming?" came a strident Scottish female voice.

"Er yes. Who is this?" I asked.

"It's the wife of the man you have been shaggin, that's who!" she barked. "Are you Angela Fleming or whit?"

"Yes. Yes, I am. But do you mind, it's 1:30 in the morning. You'll wake everyone!"

"Well, you shouldn'a be shaggin' other women's husbands should you, yer bitch!"

"I beg your pardon?"

"I've got 4 wains to feed and I'm no handing over ma husband to some snotty nosed up yer arse southerner-"

"Excuse me, I am half Scottish if you don't mind and I'm not doing anything with your husband - well, not now anyway... In any case, he told me, when I met him, that you and he had split up."

"Well we did, but-"

"Then you need to speak to him. I am no longer in the equation. Don't ring here again!" I cut her off, my heart thumping, hoping against hope that Aggie and her husband hadn't heard anything. I jumped as the phone rang again.

"Listen you whore-"

"NO!" I cut her off, left it off the hook and stuck it under the bed. After a while, I fell into a wakeful doze.

I was not sure whether it was the dogs barking or the searchlight panning across my ceiling that woke me in an instant so that I leapt out of bed and ran to the window. Down below, I could see 2 policemen and their panda car standing outside on the drive with a searchlight. I crept downstairs as quickly and quietly as I could. "Shush dogs, shush!" I hushed as I opened the front door a crack.

"Miss Flayming?" For a fleeting moment, I thought maybe I should deny being Miss Flayming.

"Yes," I squeaked.

"Do you know a Mr John Mac Allistar?"

"Yes. I used to. Not anymore. Could you, could you keep your voice down?"

"The Lothian police have contacted us as Mr Mac Allister's wife has been in touch and she says you have been... erm having an affair with him and-"

"What?"

“I’m sorry Miss. I need to ask you some questions as a matter of urgency.”

“Urgency? For goodness sake! What is this? Police have no remit to pry into a domestic.”

“We do if there is danger to human life,” he replied.

“Whose life?” I was taken aback.

“Mr Mac Allister’s. He has threatened to commit suicide if his wife prevents him from seeing you again. He left their house yesterday afternoon and has not been seen since.” For a moment, I was speechless. How the hell had my one-time affair turned into a major drama like this? The coppers looking at me in my state of undress, - hair on end, panda eyes topped off by brushed cotton pyjamas suitable for a kid of 8. They were probably wondering 'Who on earth would want to commit suicide for that?'

“Ms Flayming.”

“Fleming. It’s Fleming not Flayming,” I hissed.

"Sorry, Miss Fleming, I have to ask you, is Mr Mac Allister here?”

“No. Of course he’s not.”

“Do you think we could come in and have a look?”

“No, you absolutely can’t. The-the… the dogs will tear you apart, not to mention the owner. Really no. He’s not here and I haven’t seen him and I have no idea where he is.”

“I see." He looked at his fellow officer. “Well, thank you for your time. If you do-”

"Yes, I will but… but that woman needs to stop calling. The wife, I mean. Her.”

“I can’t promise anything,” said one.

“Try his pigeons.”

“Pigeons?”

"Yes, he has pigeons. He likes spending time with them."

The two looked at each other and shrugged. "Right."

I closed the door and locked it. Climbing back upstairs, I listened anxiously to see if Aggie and her husband had been witness to this humiliating turn of events, but thankfully, all was quiet except for the wig-lifting snores of her husband blasting out.

I was right. McAllister was with his pigeons.

I'm jolted out of my reminiscences as we pull up in the drop-off lane at Gatwick Airport. "There you go," says David as he heaves Maddie out of the back seat.

"Thank you so much, David, and please, make sure you are on time to pick us up on our return. Mungo my dog will be desperate to see me and I hate to think of him fretting even though he has Susan, my housekeeper, with him."

"Don't you worry Mrs Jensen. I will be." David loosens her grip on his arm and places the suitcases in the trolley. "Now you have a good trip."

'Thank you again, David. So kind." She smiles pathetically up at him then, turning back to me, her expression resorts to battle-axe mode.

"Right," I say brusquely. "I am going to the loo. Perhaps whilst I'm there, you can make up your mind as to how you want this holiday to go because I'm not having this nonsense any longer. I didn't call you when I said I would and that's too bad. Get over it or don't and if it's don't, we are turning round and going home right now. Ok?" I walk off.

Of course, I hope against hope she will choose 'abort' but I know that is unlikely. Maddie's disorder cannot function effectively alone. Now I am the target.

What sort of hell had the men in her personal life endured day after day I wonder, as I look at myself in the mirror. Her lover Hugo was too dim to know any better and obviously revelled in being emotionally whipped, rather like Russian women, who it appears have a saying, 'If he doesn't beat you, he doesn't love you', but poor old StJohn. I take a deep breath.

I know my fate is sealed when I am confronted with Maddie's conciliatory expression as she meets me outside. Her response fills me with doom. "Darling, I do so want us to have a nice time of course, but you must understand, I do worry so when you don't call. That's why I felt so annoyed and upset and, of course, all that business with Mungo and the fireworks."

"Right. Never mind, let's go." I smile, but I know, as sure as 'eggs is eggs', she will find the right moment on the trip when I will have to pay for my insurrection.

"Isn't it charming?" Maddie says as we walk into the foyer of a Viennese Rococo chocolate box, boutique hotel. "StJohn and I always booked in here when we came to Vienna for the opera. Now where is our concierge?" She bangs the bell on the desk then calls out. "Hello! Yooo Hoo! I say…"

A man in his early 50s appears. "Ah, you don't look like Gustav."

"No, I am not Gustav. I am Otto," he replies.

"What have you done with Gustav?"

"Nothing Madam. Gustav retired."

"Right. Well, now Otto, show us our rooms, will you? My back's killing me and I need a little rest before we go out."

Maddie's back manages to hold out until she has thoroughly examined both rooms and chosen the best for herself since, as she reminds me, she is paying. "Isn't this lovely, darling? We are right next door to one another as I asked, so I can bang on the wall and you will know to come through. Now I need 40 winks and then I'll give you a little bang when I'm ready and you can come and get me. Ok?"

"OK." I nod.

Dumping my bags on the floor of my room, I throw myself on the bed and consider the hideous prospect of the days ahead.

It strikes me that I am identical to one of those poor women in the nineteenth century who, for lack of funds, ended up being the companion to crabby old women like my aunt, but without any escape. How have I found myself in this situation? Along with ageing, lack of work, another recession that had virtually wiped me out again, I have lost status. I feel ugly and useless and my bones ache. They ache all the time. I get up and look in the mirror. My hair is gradually being allowed to turn white. I notice how it drained all colour from my face and gives me the ghostly appearance of someone who is gradually fading out of this world. How many years have I left to look forward to? Is that the right phrase? Life has become a feat of endurance not one of expectation and hope. Once I had left my 40s, which was probably my last chance to regain any kind of proper life with another partner, my world changed.

Thump! Thump! Thump! I must have fallen asleep when the noise of Maddie, banging on the wall, wakes me up. Reluctantly I drag myself up and put on my coat. Thump! Thump! I hear a muffled, "Yoo Hoo! Darling? Hurry up!"

'It's only 3 nights, you can do this, you CAN do this,' I repeat to myself as I knock on her door and walk in.

“Darling, come and sit on the bed next to me. Now, did you have a little sleep?”

“Yes. I must have drifted off.”

“Oh, I went straight off. I feel so much better for it. Now, pass me my make-up bag and I’ll just powder my snitch and then we can go. I’m so looking forward to seeing ‘Tosca’. It was StJohn’s favourite opera you know. We saw it at the Met. That’s why I called our cow Tosca of course.” I thought of the loneliness of the wretched cow she kept in the field by the lake. Year after year never seeing another member of her own species and a herd animal to boot - just so Maddie could say “Oh that’s my pet cow, Tosca.”

“It’s so nice to have my lovely niece with me now I no longer have StJohn.” She rubs my arm and I try hard not to flinch. "You can imagine it’s so hard for me being without him after all these years. Obviously, it’s easier for you because you have been alone for such a long time so you are used to it.”

(Well obviously).

“But it was kinder to let him die of the aneurysm than to have him operated on, especially when I noticed he was going a bit weird.”

“What do you mean weird?" I query.

“You know. Couldn’t remember this and that. Playing scrabble every evening, as we did, he tried to make some very strange words, and you know I couldn’t have borne it if he’d gone like Hugo.”

“I had no idea.“

“Yes. Such a shame. I always used to joke with him that I hoped we’d die in bed together after we’d made mad, passionate love, leaving the electric blanket on by mistake so that our bodily fluids made the electric blanket short and we were electrocuted.”

"Oh God."

"But don't you see, we'd be rolling in our-"

"No!" I interrupt.

Maddie laughs. "What's the matter, darling?"

"Everything. It's not right. I can't hear this. I'm your niece. Can we go now?"

"Absolutely sweetheart, just pass me my stick. Aaaaaaah!" She lets out a loud groan, like that of a wounded bison, as she levers herself off the bed. "Christ, my back. Wait a minute, wait a minute." A series of grunts accompanies her attempts to unfurl her body to an upright position. "There, done it." She smiles triumphantly. "Now you must let me take your arm when we are outside but don't when we are inside. I don't want to look disabled in front of others. Got it?"

"Yes," I agree obediently.

"Right, let's be off."

We take a taxi to an expensive, old-fashioned restaurant, all white tablecloths, silver plate candlesticks and heavy velvet drapes, where Maddie manages, despite her age and lack of exercise, to polish off a Vienna schnitzel the size of a small calf. I make an attempt to dissuade her from eating a baby animal, but it's dismissed with an irritated wave of her hand. "You cannot come to Vienna Angela, without eating a Vienna schnitzel."

"I can."

"Do as you like, but I shan't."

Apart from this small hiccough, the meal goes fairly smoothly until, prior to leaving, she grabs the white serving cloth off the elderly waiter's arm and holds it up below her eyes, like a yashmak, saying in what she deems is her best 'come hither' voice. "Ok Baby, how about you and me…?" At 82, with skin like tree bark, it is not the kind of invite that is going to stir the inhabitants of anyone's underpants, let alone a man of his age. The waiter smiles nervously and asks her if she wants the bill. Reaching out to stroke his hand, she says, "I'm just teasing". He scuttles off as fast as his old legs can carry him and a younger waiter appears with the bill minutes later.

Maddie intermittently forgets that her days of beauty and sexual attraction are long gone. Flirting had been her 'pass go'/'get out of jail card', which she had exploited from a very early age. For most women of her era, it had been their only currency. I could see it was hard for her to stop the behaviour of a lifetime, but I prayed to the gods she might give it a rest whilst with me.

Making our way to the opera house the cold is intense. Maddie grabs my arm and puts all her weight on it. Unlike her sister, my mother, she has retained a good solid bulk though she has shrunk a few inches from 5'10 to down to 5'6 as her spine, like my poor mother's, has contracted from stenosis. My bad shoulder starts to ache but, as it isn't too far to lug her, I think it best not to mention it until our return and get her to swap sides.

The opera house is suddenly hot after the freezing temperature outside. We make our way through a crush of people handing in coats, only to be confronted by a long queue stretching through to the box office. We stand in line with Maddie huffing and puffing. "How long is this going to take?" she grumbles.

"Why don't you go and sit down and I'll get the tickets?" I suggest.

"No. No. This is ridiculous." Before I can stop her, she's forging forward, batting people out of the way with her stick. “Excuse me. Let me through. Please.” I cringe as I watch her part the sea of people, hoping they won’t associate her with me. Minutes later, I hear her foghorn rise above their heads. “Angela, come here. Hurry up. I’ve got our tickets. We’re in the stalls. Come on.” A mass of angry, disgruntled faces swing round to identify me as her accomplice. I squeeze my way through trying hard to avoid eye contact.

The opera is ok. Tosca herself is fairly attractive and of a reasonable size, i.e. not ‘excessively body positive’. She sings her song of love with convincing passion so that I, and I’m sure the rest of the audience, dare to hope the object of her desire, when he appears, is going to be one gorgeous-looking hunk. To our collective disappointment, a squat bloke from Hobbiton sidles round the corner of the set to begin his lament. His voice is fine nevertheless and the first half sails by pleasantly.

Interval time.

“So now do tell me, have you any children?” I’ve been sent off to get coffee and sachertorte so have parked Maddie at a table with 2 well-dressed Viennese women in their 70s, one in a wheelchair. Maddie has immediately engaged them in conversation and I am back just in time to hear the leading question about offspring. This was her ‘go to’ strategy when first meeting strangers she wanted to impress. Both women regale her with joyful anecdotes about their adult children who visit them regularly.

“And you? Is this your granddaughter here?” The wheelchair lady asks innocently.

My aunt flashes me a look. “My granddaughter? Good God no! This is my niece.”

"Oh, I'm so sorry, forgive me," the woman apologises.

"No, no, I have 3 children," Maddie continues, taking control of the direction of travel. "Well, I say 3, but actually, (she sighs) my son died when he was 34 of kidney failure." There! She has arrived at her desired destination and gets the required response as the women's faces collapse into expressions of compassion accompanied by empathetic murmurings. Yes, it is true. My cousin had died then. His kidney disease was a result of the combination of his mother's and father's chromosomes. On a scale from 1-10, the women have reacted pretty much on the level of a 9, which is a high mark, and I thought Maddie would have been more than satisfied with the result, but I haven't taken into account the wheelchair. On reflection, a long-dead child may not have been quite enough to push my aunt to the front of the line in the victim stakes. She is nothing if not competitive. "Yes," she murmurs looking down whilst distractedly turning her cluster of emerald and diamond rings on her finger. "It was ghastly." There's a pause. She raises her head and looks directly into the eyes of the wheelchair woman. "Now I only have one daughter left as the other daughter was murdered!"

A collective gasp of horror escapes from all 3 of us. I wave my hand in the air as if batting away a nasty smell and cry out, "No! No! That's not true."

The women look shocked and then bewildered as Maddie reaches out and grabs hold of my arm wrenching me round to face her; her eyes narrow as she hisses, "Don't you dare interfere. Shut up. It's none of your business." Releasing me, she calmly picks up her fork and proceeds to eat her slice of Sachertorte. The women very quickly make their excuses and leave. All communication stops as we take our seats again for the second half, but I am unable to concentrate on anything other than the violent outburst just witnessed. How am I to manage someone who is obviously so disturbed? My hands start sweating and I can feel my heart beating abnormally. I have a whirlwind going on in my head. The face of my supposedly murdered female cousin, who I knew to be very much alive, swims in and out of my inner vision, interspersed with that of Maddie's, twisted with anger. But what was this? Another image begins to push its way through, distorting the edges, blurring the features. Maddie's face trembles and dissolves as those of my stepfather's morph into place. My old fear is back. I feel the panic rise but just as it starts to get a hold Tosca throws herself off the battlements. The opera is over. I am going to have to face the monster.

Stepping outside Maddie reaches for my arm. "Oh, sorry, can you go the other side?" I ask nicely. "It's just, it's my bad side and it's getting a bit sore."

"No. No," she replies crossly and pulls away. "I wouldn't want to put you out."

"You're not putting me out. I just need to rest a bit on that side. Here." I offer her my other arm.

"Don't bother. I can tell you don't want to help me so please leave it." She starts to wobble off across the road.

"Aunt Maddie, don't be silly. I am happy to-"

"I said leave it. I will manage. I don't want to cause you a problem. Heaven forbid." I follow her stooped back as she struggles across the cobblestones to hail a taxi, aware that she now has the opportunity she needs to turn the tables on me. I am now the guilty party and retribution is hers. On our return, Maddie goes straight to her room and shuts the door without so much as a 'Good night.'

It's late. I am lying in a hot bath. I can't sleep. The evening's events have disturbed me to such an extent that sleep is out of the question; the madness of it all and the shadow of Duncan surfacing again through the horror. I started to replay the many images of him when he was at full warp when I was eight; tiptoeing up the front stairs in order to catch me reading with my light on - towering over me, shouting his opprobrium as I lay like a terrified mouse trying to disappear under the covers; the knee jiggling the breakfast table if my fork or spoon accidentally happened to touch my teeth. "Must you sound as if you are tramping through a marsh when you are eating?"; standing behind me, signalling to my mother that I stank; his derisory laughter at anything James and I tried to create; his rage at the church bells on Sunday - flinging open the back door cursing the bell ringers; his fury at other car drivers so that his toddler son thought cars were called 'bloody bloody's'. the day he stoved in the head of our little cat - No! no! I mustn't go there. Shake my head, shake, shake - What's that noise? A telephone ringing.

MY telephone ringing!

Please God, don't let that be her. I scramble out of the bath, grab a towel and pick up my phone. No ID on the number. "Hello."

"Hello. Is that Miss Angela Fleming?" says the voice.

"Yes. Who is this?"

"I'm ringing from Southampton Hospital on behalf of your brother, Mr James Fleming."

"My brother? What's happened? Is he alright?"

"I'm afraid he has had an accident and has had to undergo emergency surgery due to a bleed on his brain."

"What? How?"

"He is in a coma. He is stable at the moment, but he has been quite unwell and is in intensive care."

"What happened?"

"They will let you know when you come in."

"You can't say? But -"

"No, I can't say. They will tell you more when you come in."

"I… I'm in Vienna at the moment. I'll get a flight back tomorrow and come straight down. Will he be alright? I mean…" I try to control the wobble in my voice.

"He is in intensive care, so we are doing our best for him, but you are aware he has a drink and drug dependency."

"Yes, yes, I do."

"Right. As I said, he is in intensive care."

"Ok. Thank you. Ermm, yes… Thank you… Thank you for letting me know."

Chapter Twenty-One
WHO?

The rain lashes down, creating a timpani of sound on the car bonnet as I drive to the hospital. Small lakes appear. I see a car ahead of me aquaplane then wobble off onto the hard shoulder. Skies marbled with grey and dirty-coloured clouds overshadow the fields which lie empty and sodden. The only sign of life in the deluge are the swollen rivers and streams which rush through the land in a hurry to empty their extra burden to the sea.

"Excuse me, I'm looking for my brother, James Fleming. I was told he was in here?" The nurse looks up.

"That's right. The bed next to the door."

"No. That's not James," I reply, shaking my head.

The nurse looks puzzled. I follow her to the bed. She picks up the chrome board clamped on the end. "James Fleming. See. He's been in an induced coma. The surgeon will be coming around soon. He'll be able to let you know more."

I stare at the wasted carcass of an old man wired up to drips and machines, his head bandaged, his eyes sunken into a weathered face hollowed out by addiction, lined by struggle and misery. I sit down on the chair next to the bed. His hand lay above the sheets, swollen and red. I reach out and place my own on top of it. "James, it's Angela."

Chapter Twenty-Two
CARE IN MY COMMUNITY

I am a carer. I care for my brother though I don't live with him. I care for my dear old horse Purdie, and now my cats. I have friends who I can tell are hoping I can care for them and now I get paid to be a carer for someone's mother with middling dementia. Her name is Stella. Once again acting work has gone into hibernation where I am concerned, so this is the alternative. I have discovered, after lessons learnt from training problem horses for several years, that I have finally got a level of patience that can endure the repetitive conversation of someone with dementia for at least 3 hours before I need a break.

It's a summer's day and finally, the rain has stopped. There was a time in April when I thought it would never cease. Like in the 14 Century when it rained for 2 years, triggering the Great Famine, closely followed by the plague. As Shakespeare said: 'When sorrows come, they come not in single spies but in battalions.' Certainly did for them.

Looking down over a bucolic Surrey landscape with the sun spreading a primrose yellow light on the fields, drying out the drenched earth, I can just hear the meanderings of Stella's confused mind in the building behind me. I've left her happily repeating herself out loud, as she reads and re-reads the inscriptions etched on the interior of the small, circular mausoleum. Built with local bricks and decorated with pre-Raphaelite angels, it's a thing of great beauty and I know it'll confine her safely. I've awarded myself a good 5-minute break from the incessant, repetitive statements such as:

"How unusual, houses made of brick," "When you die you just go to sleep," / "My husband would have loved you. He loved tall, blonde, thin girls." Yes, I am still tall, thin and blonde but, according to the acting world, I am unemployable because I am 'old'. I have retained my figure and I have dyed my white hair back to dark blonde so it no longer drains the life out of me. Even though I am 'old,' I'm not Mr Kipling-cake-granny-old, so I don't fit into the stereotypical concept of an older woman. I don't bumble along like Miriam Margolyes farting openly at the drop of a hat to the delighted disgust of millions of television viewers. I am in the category of 'old' because of my age but not my appearance.

Now, for all those Pollyanna types out there who tell you that they aren't in the slightest bit bothered by the thump of the Saga magazine as it lands on the doormat, welcoming you to the era of the ancient and frail, they are bloody liars! Even if you lack ambition, for the majority of single and or abandoned women smiling crookedly out from the magazines, trying to look 'bright' after their ghastly makeovers, you cannot afford to. This is because they've taken our bloody pensions away until we women are practically face down on the mattress and probably not worth reviving. You still have to graft though no one wants to employ you. So you buy up every wrinkle lotion, eye bag corrector, age spot eradicator you can get your hands on because you must not look too old; old in this country, as a single woman, is tantamount to being an 'untouchable'.

"Seen enough Stella?" I ask as I watch her from the doorway spinning round and round, chasing the writing.

"Oh yes, yes, I have. Goodness, I'm quite dizzy!" She staggers to one side.

"Steady!" I grab her before she hits the deck. Maybe I had left her a little too long.

"Isn't it marvellous though?" she coos. "And all made of brick. So unusual."

"Yes. All made of brick," I repeat wearily. "Shall we go and get some tea?"

"Oh yes, darling. Good idea. Although, no cake for me."

"Of course," I agree, knowing full well she will have cake and plenty of it.

Stella, a lover of fashion, a one-time beauty (and still beautiful), a semi-anorexic and an actress the size of a pixie, had spent a lifetime denying herself sugary treats, but now her mind was blown, she ate them with gusto. Her eyes bulged with pleasure when they alighted on chocolate brownies or the array of sweets at the checkout, adding them to the basket with an, "I know it's very naughty, but a little treat every now and then never hurt anybody." In actual fact, it was a lot more than every now and then. Once back home, the sweets were secreted into every little cubby hole she could find, her former guilt propelling her behaviour once more. At night, she would interrupt her television viewing, which went on till nearly 2 in the morning, with raids on the sequestered places, scrabbling in the darkest corners, trying to remember where she had stowed her treasure. Like a rat, her addiction was spot on, informing her there was sugar to be had nearby, but her mind struggled to locate it.

"Stella," I say as I watch her spreading a slab of butter on a scone. "I hope you don't mind, but tomorrow we will have to go over to Hampshire to my brother's old flat as the council want it back and it needs cleaning and clearing. Are you ok with that? It's just that it can't be done any other time."

"Of course, darling. I don't mind at all. Do whatever you like. Whatever you need to do is ok by me." She launches the scone missile, now piled high with cream and jam, into her mouth, leaving a frothy moustache behind.

"Oh good. Thank you, Stella. I'm afraid it might be a bit boring."

"Not at all," she replies, smiling. "I never get bored. Life is far too wonderful ever to be bored."

James had survived but at a cost. Since returning from Vienna, I had been travelling down the motorway to the hospital on a daily basis. He had come out of the coma and then relapsed as he struggled through a lung infection and 'C difficile'. Emaciated to the point where his muscles could no longer support him, he was given a mattress on the floor in a private room so he could crawl around if need be, which he did, trying to escape the 'horrible black things' that crept around the edges of the skirting board or the 'Indian man' who was trying to knife him! He was like a bewildered animal taken from the wild and caged. He seemed to half-recognise me but he could no longer speak properly and was unable to communicate in a cohesive way.

I had been there just the day before and found myself having to feed him as the nurse said she was too busy. Trying hard not to gag, I spooned food into James' toothless mouth as he blinked up at me, his hands twitching the sheets. Every now and then, he lifted them up in the air miming rolling a cigarette. My phone buzzed. "Hello, it's Fran here. James's friend. From the post office." The voice sounded educated and unsure.

"Hello. Yes, I got your text. It's very good of you to help out. Are you sure you have time?"

"Yes, yes. My partner is going to run the post office whilst I'm with you and the lady downstairs, James's neighbour, has offered to help too. I'll be there Thursday at 10.30. Ok?"

"Oh, that is so kind," I replied. "I have no idea what kind of a state the flat is in, I have to warn you. Anyway, see you then."

"Yes. See you then."

I smiled at James. "That was Fran, your friend," I said, hoping for some recognition. He stared back at me uncomprehendingly. "She's going to help me with your flat."

Chapter Twenty-Three
THE FIFTH LABOUR OF HERACLES

Helping Stella out of the car, I steer her in the direction of the concrete steps leading to James's flat. It looks just as unwelcoming as it has ever done but worse as the folk across the way have left piles of junk outside their door.

"Ok, now Stella, stay close won't you?"

"Yes, darling," she nods obediently.

"I mean, don't wander off will you, because I don't want to lose you."

"No, darling." She shakes her head and follows me like a small lap dog. I push the door open against the weight of a mound of junk mail and immediately, the smell hits me.

"Oh God, where is that coming from?" Nervously, I make my way down the narrow hall. The door to the bathroom is ajar. I poke my head round. I'm confronted with excrement smeared all over the walls and floor. I let out an involuntary cry of horror and, grabbing the handle, pull the door too. "Oh no!"

"What is it, darling?" Stella looks at me with alarm.

"Don't go in there, whatever you do Stella!"

"No, no, I shan't if you say so. But what is it?"

"Can't you smell it?" I ask, my hand over my nose, trying not to retch.

"No, darling. I can't smell a thing. I lost my sense of smell ages ago."

"Lucky you. Well, it's... erm... well, very unhygienic. Something must have gone wrong with the lavatory." I move swiftly on and step into the sitting room. It is ankle-high in newspapers, junk mail, cigarette ends, books, old wine bottles filled with urine - yes urine - all coated in a thick layer of dust. There is an even larger burn in the centre of the stained carpet. Two outdated televisions are stacked on top of one another alongside an equally outdated stereo system and an old armchair, its seat partially collapsed. It sits under the grimy windows which are so grimy, the light struggles to get in. "Oh God!"I groan.

"Oh dear," says Stella. "This is a bit of a mess isn't it?"

"Hello!" a voice calls out. "Hello." A woman in her 50s appears wearing an apron with a Jessica Rabbit body printed on the front. "Hello, I'm Fran. From the post office. Goodness, this is a bit of a mess, isn't it?"

"That's just what I said," chirrups Stella.

"I'm so sorry Fran," I apologise. "I don't think I can ask you to help me with this it's too... too much really."

"Oh no, no, it's fine," she says, putting a brave face on it as she glances down at the wine bottles of piss, not sure if it's fermenting wine though something tells her it really IS fermenting piss. "I had no idea he was in such a state. He never invited anyone in and now I know why. Goodness me."

"Yes. I haven't seen the bedrooms yet," I reply. "Stella, you stay here whilst we have a look, and please don't touch anything will you?" This last request seems unnecessary but there is no telling what she might do with a brain that has a mind of its own.

"Of course, darling. I won't touch a thing," she assures me.

Bedroom number one is cold and damp with the window half covered in cardboard where the pane is smashed but otherwise messy with clothes, books and bits and pieces once belonging to our mother. Bedroom number two is another case of well... 'number twos'. This time in the bed, on the sheets and crusting the seat of a pair of jeans and some old pants. “Fran,” I say, mortified. “I really cannot ask you to do this.”

But she does. They do. Fran, and the neighbour who lives below, buckle down in their aprons and rubber gloves and, leaving the bathroom to the county's environmental health action group, they help clear and clean most of the sitting room and some of the foulest bedroom. Water has to be boiled and ferried up from downstairs since the water has been cut off from non-payment of the bill, which I discover later, as I tear my way through endless letters of debt threats in amongst gambling investments with promises of huge winnings. Slipped in amongst them is a note in an almost illegible scrawl, offering James some heroin and quaaludes at a knockdown price. Obviously, the friendly dealer had a sale on.

“Stella! Not in there!” I shout as I hear her trying to open the door to the bathroom.

“Ok, darling,” comes the cheery reply, but she's at it again 5 minutes later.

“No. Stella, what did I say!” I exclaim. I hear the panic in her small footsteps as she hurries off down the hallway. “Oh no.” I get up from the floor where I've been cleaning out the contents of a filthy drawer. As my only income is Stella, I cannot afford to lose her. No pension and unemployable as an actress, weakened by the abundance of menopause, I find myself scratching around for any job to keep me alive. It's been a lifetime since my mother tried to bring up 3 children, ill from poverty, abuse and stress, with little help from the state and almost none from the separate fathers who weren't legally obliged to give any. Here I am, decades later, having worked all my life, paid my taxes, and am singled out as the gender once again that has to forfeit. It must still be lodged in the minds of politicians that the nuclear family is the only one to be considered, that the thousands of single women who don't live off the larger wage packets of men are to be sidelined and ignored. These are the ones who work all their lives and near the end are there to look after everyone; the ailing parents and, in my case, the broken brother. No time off for good behaviour. No realistic help.

"Stella! Stella!" I hurry after her and nearly collide with Fran coming up the stairs, heaving a bucket of hot water.

"I just saw her heading into the fields over there." She gesticulates with her head.

"Thanks," I say and run off after her. Stella is already busily absorbed in one of her favourite pastimes, picking up leaves and marvelling at their construction.

"Look at this, darling," she says as I catch up with her, an expression of wonder on her face as she holds up an oak leaf. "Isn't it beautiful? My, my, but nature is such a clever thing. Now if there were a God, and I don't think for one minute there is, he did a very good job when he made these, don't you agree?"

"Yes. Lovely. Perhaps we can take some to the flat and look at them there?" I suggest, picking up some random leaves and handing them over to her. "Maybe you could make a collage?"

"Now that's a good idea," she says and I manage to steer her back to the noxious-smelling flat, settling her in a corner as I sort through some old photos at the bottom of the drawer.

I pull out an old black and white photo of James and myself in our early 20s, standing side by side, looking at something out of the picture. As unalike as brother and sister could possibly be. Both tall, but James muscle-strong with dark hair and a hard stare. I myself, almost sweet with light brown hair, looking as if butter wouldn't melt. Such disguises. Our lives ahead of us, but the short lives lived already chaotic and besmirched. I sigh, putting the photo into an envelope with others and look around at the mess. The task of cleaning the place is Herculean.

James's loneliness and desolation are implicit in every part of the flat. The kitchen fungal with rotting food and cupboards full of tins that date from another era, complete the picture of someone who had given up on a future and haunted by a past. "Need a little break?" My thoughts are interrupted by Fran and the neighbour bringing in mugs of tea and a pack of digestive biscuits.

"Yes. Wonderful, thanks." I hand a mug to Stella who is excited by the biscuits.

"I know it's naughty but-" She reaches out to claim one, then, on second thoughts, takes 2, then settles back down on the floor with a happy smile.

"How is James?" asks the neighbour, a steady-looking woman in her early 50s.

"Better. Well... better-ish. I've got him out of hospital and into a very good rehab unit. If they had watched him when he was admitted, he wouldn't have fallen off the bed and smashed his head open and he would be able to speak properly. He's on 24-hour watch now as he's paranoid, but he is eating much more as long as the helper eats with him so he doesn't think he's being poisoned. But you know, it's an improvement. Not sure if he will ever be able to talk well again but we shall see. Early days." They both nod earnestly and I smile back. I omit to tell them I have had to have him sectioned.

"Does he remember me?" asks Fran.

"Can't really say. It's difficult because, as I say, his speech is all over the place. He thinks he's perfectly lucid but it all sounds like gobbledey gook."

"Such a shame." She shakes her head. "He was so clever. I think James went properly downhill after the death of his friend - that girl. I don't know if you knew about that?"

"Yes. I knew about her."

Oh, yes. I knew about that girl. My agent, who I had not heard from for months, rang out of the blue. 'Hurrah!' I thought. At last! But instead of being sent for an audition, she informed me that the police wanted to speak to me about my brother. As my stomach lurched in time-honoured fashion, I found myself hopping from one leg to the other - my shell-shock response. The first time it occurred was when James had come to see me for the day. Just as lunch was ready, he disappeared into the bathroom to jack up, under the pretence of having a tummy ache. I stood outside the bathroom door in a panic, wondering how to cope if he overdosed; whether I'd be able to break the door down in time. As I waited, I became aware that I was hopping from foot to foot in a weird little dance, like the men who suffered shell shock after the First World War.

"Hello Officer, it's Angela Fleming. I believe you wished to speak to me about my brother, James Fleming."

"Hello. Yes. This is concerning an incident at the Rowley Estate. A young woman has died."

Pause.

"What?"

"Mr Fleming was with her at her flat and it appears they were drinking together. She fell down the stairs and broke her neck. I wanted to ask you a few questions about your brother. Would you say he has a violent nature?"

Pause.

"Are you saying my brother murdered the woman? Is that what you are saying?"

"He is a suspect at the moment."

The idea that my brother was a murderer was beyond believable.. My brother, the murderer? No! That was going one step too far. "My brother would never do that. Never! He's not a murderer. He… he, he isn't like that. He has his troubles and, as you probably realise, he drinks and, and… no! He wouldn't have hurt her. There must have been an accident."

Accident. Yes. It was an accident…..

"Yes," I repeat. "I knew about the girl.

"I think," Fran continues, "James went very badly downhill after the girl's death because you see, the whole estate turned against him. He was an outsider with that accent of his, obviously being an educated man. Very polite and charming. Kept himself to himself, but after the incident with the woman, well, he was pretty much alone. Obviously, I would see him in the village post office and Jonathan, our vicar, always kept in touch. But I could tell he was drinking much, much more."

"She was a troubled girl that one," adds the neighbour. "She was in a wheelchair. Been in a car crash when she was younger. I think she was in pain a lot of the time. Hence the drinking."

"He wasn't found guilty. It was definitely an accident," I state.

"Yes. He's a gentle soul underneath, but so lonely. Be nice if he had someone else he could turn to. Is your father still with us?" Fran asks.

"Our father? No. They were estranged for many years, I think James's demise also had a lot to do with that. The collapse of his relationship with Dad and then…"

"Ah, I see. Yes, that's tough," sighs Fran and the neighbour nods in agreement.

"Yes. Boys need a dad."

"Does anyone want that last biscuit?" asks Stella, her eyes fixed on it like a hungry dog.

Fran picks up the plate. "I think Stella does." Stella giggles and reaches out to claim it.

Chapter Twenty-Four
LIAR, LIAR, PANTS ON FIRE!

1990's

On the journey home, it's too late for me to cook, so we stop off at a fish and chippy. Being a vegetarian, Stella has some deep-fried pea and potato croquettes and we share a paper cone of hot, salted and vinegary soggy chips. Sitting in the car, the windscreen misted up with the hot steam, she turns to me, a large floppy chip hovering in front of her mouth. "Ooh, this is such fun. I haven't eaten chips in paper for years and years."

"Stella, I feel very bad not getting you back home in time to cook you a meal."

"Oh, darling, this is so much better. Don't get me wrong, I like your cooking very much, but this is a real treat."

Setting off again, I switch on the radio so that I can listen to the babbling of some idiot presenter in an effort to blot out the horror of the day. The question raised about my father by Fran triggers a vivid memory of our last meeting when I travelled down to see him after a period of non-communication. I was very apprehensive about the meeting since there had been a falling out with Joan (his second wife) which had resulted in my being excommunicated on her orders. Eventually, Dad broke ranks and made it up with me, much to her annoyance.

Over the years, I had watched Joan keep my father to heel with her emotional outpourings, of which he lived in terror. Through sheer force of tears, tantrums and sulks, she managed to control him. Her self-induced sense of inferiority would from time to time, flare up, like an episode of IBS, and she would invariably have an episode when I came into the picture. My presence challenged her authority over him and little imagined slights were forever on her radar so that being in her company was wearing.

Little Dad (he was now, having shrunk with age, still retaining his compact figure) greeted me with a shy smile at the door and a bear hug. "Hello, hello," he said, laughing nervously.

"Hello, Daddy," I replied.

"Go through." He gestured toward the sitting room. "Joan is in there."

'The Kraken awaits' I thought and stepped into her den.

Joan managed a forced smile and a butterfly kiss on the cheek. "Do you know where James is, Angela?" was her first question. Not waiting for a reply, she continued in hushed tones. "Because you know, you and James are getting some money when your father dies through your grandmother's trust - I think it's about £20,000 - and I mean, I don't know what James will do with it."

"Sorry?"

"I mean, after all, I won't have anything when your father goes and James will just spend it on drugs won't he?"

"20,000 Quid! That's nice I didn't know we were getting anything," I said.

"Yes, you are, but I won't will I?"

"Well, no, I suppose not. Since you aren't her grandchild I don't suppose you will, but you and Dad got her house with all the antiques and her savings. Has that all been spent?"

"That was some time ago."

"Ok. But I presume though you have a pension, Dad's pension and also this house?"

"Yes but-"

"I'm sorry Joan, Granny left the money to us grandchildren. If James wants to stick it in his veins it's entirely down to him, don't you think?"

"Well, I think it's a waste," she muttered, sitting back on her chair, looking angrily out onto the garden.

Dad appeared holding a willow pattern plate with a pile of carefully trimmed sandwiches, neatly stacked one on top of another. "I thought you might be hungry so I made you some sandwiches." He offered them to me with pride.

"Oh Dad, I'm sorry I ate before I left to come down here," I said apologetically.

"He made them especially for you." Joan eyed me disapprovingly.

"I'll have some a bit later. They look delicious. Thanks."

"No, no, That's ok. You just have what you feel like." He placed the plate on the coffee table and sat next to Joan so they faced me, side by side. "You ok, are you?' he asked.

"Yes." I nodded. "Fine."

"Good. Good." He nodded back.

"Shall I tell her or will you?" Joan asked.

"No. I will. Ermm… Angela, I wanted you to know that I am having to go in for an operation for an aneurysm. It's a big operation and… well, I... you never know with these things."

I was taken aback. "That's what Uncle StJohn had."

"Yes. He chose not to go in for the operation, didn't he?"

“And look what happened to him,” Joan said, pulling a face. “I can’t live without your father. He’s got to have the operation.”

“Otherwise?” I asked.

“Well… there is no real warning but yes, it will happen, you know, if they don’t operate…” he trailed off.

“But did they say when? When it might occur?”

“No, no. It could be tomorrow or it could be in 12 months’ time. They can’t tell exactly.” I looked down at the rug. It had a floral motif round the edges. Pale pink and blue. “Plenty of people who are in good health, like myself, do well with the operation.” He tried to sound reassuring.

“Yes, they do,” chimed in Joan. “In any case, he’s going to have it. He must have it.” Dad smiled unconvincingly. In shock, I asked questions about the operation, the hospital, the recovery time, covering up the sense of loss that was already assembling itself in my mind. Dad going to die? How could this be? My father was strong. He was almost never ill. He was like an ox. He climbed to the base camp of the Matterhorn when he was in his late 60s. An army man, a major, a paratrooper, he got the military cross… he would be fine. How could this carry him away?

“So, I was wondering.” He averted his gaze, pulling nervously at the crease in his trousers. "I was wondering if… if you knew where James was? I… er… I."

“No,” I interrupted. “No. I haven’t seen him for a long time. He didn’t want to keep in contact, so I left it. The last time I spoke to him, he said he’d be in touch when he felt like it.”

“Oh. I see.” My father looked crestfallen.

I suddenly felt angry. James was his son. Why didn’t he find him? How come it had taken him 30 years to decide he wanted to contact him at a time which might cause James the greatest distress? Why should I be the one to go looking for him, to drag him out of some heroin-induced stupor in an attempt to get him to see his father who, I knew, was a large part of the problem.

Joan smiled knowingly. "Well, I don't know. I mean, what is it with James? What is his problem? I don't understand."

I thought, maybe now is the time for her, for both of them, to understand. Maybe, this was the moment of truth. Once Dad remarried, he had become ensconced in other lives; bringing up her children from her first marriage so that James and I, at the age of 12, had become his part-time children. My father had been aware of some of the awful places we had lived in along with the constant lack of money, but whether he was aware of the holy horror we lived in under the persecution of Duncan I wasn't sure. I supposed he had another family to consider, and in any case, it was way outside his capacity to deal with so nothing was ever discussed. The distance grew between us over the years. The secrets and the hurt hidden away. As I watched my father grow older and less capable, I had no wish to cause him unhappiness; but I had stayed mute too often so that Joan had become emboldened and now she was after James' small inheritance. I wasn't having it. I watched her sitting in her chair, playing to the gallery with her fake concern. You really want to know?"

"Yes," she almost sneered.

'Fasten your seat belt,' I thought and, taking a deep breath, I focused on the carpet and launched into a brief, horrible history of James's life. Starting with our return from Malaya to England finding ourselves with Victorian grandparents locked in the kitchen garden behind chicken wire to the orphanage she dumped us in and then a concise run through all the way to the last time I had spoken to him several years back. I could see with my peripheral vision, moments when my father wriggled in his seat or shook his head in discomfort (or was it denial). I didn't linger apart from when emotional recall forced me to stop, swallow and collect myself. Other than that, I managed to steer a course as a matter of fact as the shipping forecast. Reaching the end, I looked up to see the two of them frozen in their seats, staring at me as if I was something out of a horror movie. It was somewhat disconcerting, so I looked back down at the rug.

Silence.

Joan broke it first. "Do you know Angela, you've been in this house for over 45 minutes and all you've done is talk about yourself."

Rising out of my seat, I walked over and looked down at her as she shrunk back in her chair, squinting up at me like a cornered shrew. "You are… you are (I wasn't sure what to call her - a vile bitch, a monstrous witch, a fucking cunt) a very, very unpleasant woman."

She looked over at my father, hoping for backup, but he appeared to be in a state of petrification. Jumping to her feet, she dived for the door shouting, "I am not an unpleasant woman. I'm not!" She ran off down the hall, thumping up the stairs and then slamming into her bedroom.

Silence again.

Awkward silence.

Dad looked as if he had been super glued to the chair. "I'm so sorry Dad. She did ask me."

“No. No. It’s… erm… no, it’s fine.”

I sat back down. “Dad. I don’t blame you. I wasn’t saying this to blame anyone.”

“No, of course, I understand.” He shook his head. He looked helpless sitting there crossing and uncrossing his ankles.

“I know you hate this sort of stuff. I’m really sorry, but I don’t know where James is.”

“Ok.”

“And you know, even if Joan and I don’t see eye to eye, I have always said how glad I am that she loves you and looks after you. You do know that.” He nodded. I looked at the plate of sandwiches. He would have given them a lot of thought; the type of filling, crusts on or off; how to best please me and now – now, it was all blown apart. I got up.

"I think I’d better go,” I said. He followed on as I walked into the hall. Stopping at the bottom of the stairs I turned to him. "I hope everything goes alright with the operation Daddy, let me know when you are going in and-”

“I am NOT an unpleasant woman!” Joan’s voice choking with emotion rang out as she made her way down the stairs, clutching a tissue. “If I’m such an unpleasant woman, why is it that my children and my grandchildren don’t think I’m unpleasant? They love me. They don’t think I’m unpleasant.” The way she kept on repeating ‘unpleasant’ I was really glad I hadn’t called her an FC.

“That’s because you aren’t ‘unpleasant’ to them, are you?" I retorted. "They’re yours. James and I are imposters. Isn’t that the truth? If you really cared about James, why did you query his inheritance from Granny?” She darted a look at Dad.

"What's this?" he asked bewildered.

"I didn't," she snapped. "That's a lie!"

"Joan, you know you did. Only half an hour ago."

"She's lying."

"Why would I lie? I didn't even know we were getting anything," I laughed.

"She's lying, John."

"John! What's with the John name? My father's name is Robert, not John! Why did you have to change his name? Is it because you couldn't bear Dad to have any other life apart from the one you had with him? Anyone or anything that came before had to be erased or disparaged, including my mother, who had nothing whatsoever to do with you. As for the last letter I received, supposedly written by my father telling me that I was such a horrid, jealous person that he had to cut me off, that was your doing, wasn't it?"

"Your father wrote that letter."

"Dictated then rubber-stamped by you. No. No. I've had enough. I can't do this. Dad, I'm sorry. This is not what I wanted to happen. I have to go. If you want to talk to James, then you will have to find him yourself. Sorry."

'MISSING'.
Missing in action.
Missing, presumed dead.
Missing are people cut loose from their family ties.
Missing are the ties that should act as a lifeline.
Missing because you thought no one cared for you.

MISSING is the name of the site that I type in James's name, birthdate and last address.

MISSING

MY BROTHER JAMES WHO I HAVE HAD NO CONTACT WITH FOR 7 YEARS.

I HAVE SOME IMPORTANT INFORMATION FOR HIM CONCERNING HIS FATHER.

IF ANYONE KNOWS OF HIS WHEREABOUTS, PLEASE CONTACT ME.

"Angela?"

"Yes."

"It's me, James."

"James?"

"Yes."

"James, where have you been?"

"Around."

Pause.

"Are you ok?"

Silence.

"Are you?"

"Yes… yes. What did you want to say to me?"

"It's Dad."

"Oh. What about him?"

"I… He had an operation and… and it didn't work. He died, James."

Beat.

"James?"

A howl of anguish.

Then the line goes dead. ……..

The sound of a loud horn blaring breaks through my reminiscences.. "You stupid fucking cow! You nearly bloody went into me!"

"Sorry!" Imouth. The man pulls away shouting obscenities.

"Stella. Are you ok?"

"Yes, dear. I'm fine. Don't you worry about me."

I pull into her drive and help her down the steps to the front door. "Well, darling, I know it wasn't very nice in the flat with all the mess and stuff, but I have had a lovely day. Such nice ladies."

"Yes. Yes, they were very nice."

"James must be very lucky to have such nice people to help him." She smiles up at me. "Isn't life wonderful?"

Chapter Twenty-Five
THE FINAL VISITATION

Looking out over a lake. Hills rise and fall in soft folds on either side. It's late afternoon on a summer's day. Moored to a post, a raft piled high with furniture, rocks gently on the lightly rippling water. I look up and see my father. He smiles down at me, expecting me to join him. I am unsure. The lake stops being a lake as it heads out between a gap in the hills and moves onto where? A sea? A raging river? Or maybe just another huge, eternal lake? "Where is it going?" I ask. My father looks into the distance and then back at me. He chuckles.

"That's for us to find out."

Do I want to find out?

Do I have a choice?

I step on board and see my brother James sitting on the lower part. My father unhooks the mooring, picks up a long paddle and pushes us away from the shore. The raft slowly moves off in the silence of the afternoon. The soft slap of water is all that can be heard as we three, united again, sail off towards the unknown, steered by my father. Fear slips away as the warm air of the summer's afternoon imbues my being. I feel safe. Safe only in dreams...

Slowly, I come to. Birds outside are signalling the dawn, rousing me from the comfort of the dream. I pull myself up to a sitting position as I try to energise myself for the day ahead. I slip on my dressing gown and follow my cats downstairs.

Kettle clicks on.

Sound of cats eating their food.

I sit at the kitchen table and stare into space.

"Morning." My lodger appears. "Coffee?"

"No thanks. Got tea." I watch her as she tidies last night's washing up away then leans against the sink sipping her drink. "I watched that programme last night you told me about," I say with a grimace.

"And?"

An image of a woman in her late twenties, sitting on a lavatory with her legs open, flips into view. "Is it my age that makes me think that seeing people on lavatories and wiping themselves is not really an intrinsic element of a drama?" I ask.

She laughs. "It's reality I suppose."

"So can be picking your nose and eating it or sniffing your pants, or inspecting the stool you just passed. It just seems there is a type of reality nowadays that people are interested in. The 'grim reality' that I experienced as a member of the 'yoof' was primarily based on dramas like 'Angela's Ashes' or 'Cathy Come Home', where people suffered from real poverty and struggled to actually survive. I mean, after being privy to the woman evacuating on the lavatory whilst smoking weed with her gay flatmate, we were later transported to a party where our heroine meets a man through a drugged and drunken haze and, in the process of having sex, he removes a blood infused tampon from her vagina and asks permission to inspect the blood clot before seriously getting down to it."

"Oh God, I know! It was pretty gross." She pulls a face. "But then, I watched a woman clip her toenails opposite me on the underground."

"Jesus! What is this? Is there no dividing line between a public and private space?"

I suppose I am like all older generations experiencing what all past generations do, once the fire of my own youth has dissipated. I imagine my granny, born in the 1890s, dying in the 1980s, would have found it even more incomprehensible. Did she feel like me, I wonder? Drifting further and further away from this world, everything tilted at an angle whereby I cannot get a footing.

I make a fresh cup of tea, open the back door and follow the cats out into the garden as they race to the bottom. I inhale the smell of a young summer's day, fresh from the cool of the night.

I am off to see James again where he is living on the south coast. I do this twice a week if I can. It's a two-and-a-half-hour round trip, sometimes more if I take him out somewhere, which I usually do. James had had a series of fits. Having his first major fit on the floor of the post office, then another in the ambulance. he was then put into a bed in intensive care where it appears the nurse didn't care. He got up off the bed, had another fit, crashed to the floor hitting his head on the protruding metal bits of the bed. The noise alerted the nurse, finally, and so they 'glued him up' (their words not mine) and put him back on the bed. Half an hour later, he got off the bed, walked out of the ward where he collapsed again. Again, they put him back on the bed where, some hours later, checked on him and realised things were not good. He was then taken down to Southampton at 2 in the morning where they operated on him. Too late for his speech, it seemed.

After I pressed to get him into a rehab unit when he was finally able to walk and feed himself, he was then dumped in a flat, in a soulless sheltered home. It's on the second floor at the end of an empty, sanitised corridor. Here he is supposed to look after himself. Help is sparse and is only provided to get him to take his pills and give him pocket money, but it's essentially a place for the decrepit and brain-challenged. He knows no one; everything is unfamiliar and the damage to his brain has affected his capacity to string meaningful words together. The thought of him alone in the stark sheltered flat, back on the booze, pains me. He sets off every day on the three-quarters of a mile-long walk to the local Sainsburys to buy his small bottle of vodka. I cannot stop him and I cannot blame him.

I pick up my cup of tea and look out onto the garden. I wonder what mood I will find him in today. The bay tree cutting he gave me is now a large bush and my garden, from what was just a scrappy bit of wasteland when I first moved in, is now a collage of colour. James's skill with plants and his love of nature is present in the garden which he helped me with, once in a while, before he went missing.

"Now listen here Angela, you are the main queen. Do you understand the yicketty yacketty base movement of this assumption?" James looks at me expectantly. He requires an answer.

All I can say is, "Yes."

"Gotcha. So when the baldness of the main female in the line, such as you, hmm... which is the yicketty of all the purposes then you, my... hmmm... Queen, you have to do the right thing because you are the main female of the line."

"Yes," I say again.

James sits on the sofa surrounded by cigarette papers, sweet wrappers and tanin-stained mugs of tea. He starts to roll another cigarette with careful precision, stopping every now and then to take a sip from the mug which he assures me is just coffee but we both know is laced with vodka. I know I have about 10 maybe 15 more minutes before he will start to refuse to do anything.

"James, how about we give your hair a wash?' I suggest.

"I hate this fucking detrimental," he says. "It's a fucking… up the worst it could. Shit houses. Where are trees for my air?"

"I know. I'm sorry. I am trying to find somewhere in the countryside for you."

Even at his old flat, he had the solace of looking out onto a landscape of fields and trees, but here there are just roofs, the only birdsong being the plaintive mew of seagulls wheeling overhead, carried in from the sea.

Unable to read any longer or work out how to turn an oven on or put a plugin, his life has become a minefield of emptiness. Twice he's run away. He was found in someone's garden at 2 in the morning, taken to hospital and absconded again. I believe somewhere, under all the confusion, his true self tried to make a last-ditch attempt to take control, to try to get back to his old home. A taxi driver, whom he flagged down to take him there, rang the police when he realised halfway, that James had no money to pay him. That James was unable to speak properly and looked like a homeless person hadn't deterred the man from picking him up.

"Miss Fleming, it's Baymede Hospital here. I believe we have your brother, a Mr James Fleming." I raced to the hospital. I saw him before he saw me, sitting in a chair by the side of a bed, his head bowed as he fiddled with a matchstick, muttering unintelligibly to himself. He was still wet and smelled slightly fungal. When he saw me, the look of relief on his face was hard to bear. "James, it's ok. I'm here."

"I am diddle and disdainful journeying too far Angela."

"Yes. I know. You're all wet. We must get you back and get some dry clothes. And something to eat."

"May I have a word with you, Miss Fleming?" The doctor appeared at the door.

"James, I will be 5 minutes. You stay there and I will be back, ok? Then we'll go. Don't move now, I promise I'll just be a few minutes. Stay there, alright?"

The doctor took me to another room. "Just to put you in the picture Miss Fleming, your brother as you know is an alcoholic?"

"Yes," I replied.

"We would normally give someone with his addiction medication to prevent him fitting but, as it is, he refuses to let us do that. We cannot force him but, unless he either has the medication or some more alcohol, very soon he will start having fits."

"Right."

"So, this may sound a bit contrary to all medical advice, but I suggest, on your way home, you buy some alcohol and give it to him straight away. What does he drink normally?"

"Vodka."

"Well he has been without any for quite a long period of time now, so he's probably got about 10 minutes or so before the fitting will begin."

"Ok." I nodded, silently panicking.

I herded James out of the hospital in double quick time and made a beeline for the nearest shop. The local Tesco only had a large bottle of vodka, so I bought a bottle of water, chucked it away and decanted most of the vodka into it. I gave James the actual vodka bottle otherwise he wouldn't believe me and refused to drink water. Handing it to him, he looked at me like a naughty child. "Oh… not allowed?"

"Yes, allowed." I nodded. "Get it down you or the doctor said you will have a fit and I'm not good with that sort of thing." He happily obeyed.

Now James has given up trying. His life has become the vodka and he's kept on a 1/2 bottle a day. Every day, he collects the exact change I leave for him with the carer. At around 10.30 in the morning, he takes his money, then sets off. Sometimes he cannot wait to get home before imbibing and I have found him on a couple of occasions, sitting in the bus shelter, gulping it down, jabbering to himself. Despite being caught stealing from Sainsbury's a few times, the staff are terribly nice to him. The woman often at the till listens to his nonsense smiling warmly, sometimes reaching over with a friendly pat on his hand. The kindness of ordinary hard-working people has surprised me; these being the deplorable ones who the liberal left despise for voting for Brexit.

I put the potatoes on to steam, boil the water for some spinach and arrange the salmon in readiness under the grill. I look round the edge of the door to see what James is up to. "Shit fucking whatsit." He removes the cap he wears and scratches his head. The large dent where they had to drill through the front of his skull remains hairless. His fingers cease scratching as they feel the dip and he frowns, perplexed.

"Do you remember how you got that James?" I ask. He pulls a face. "You had a fit in the post office and your friend Fran - remember her?"

"Ermm… Fran the woman. Now, she is the queen of the female line, as is the blessing."

"Right. Well, Fran called an ambulance and they took you to hospital but unfortunately, they didn't watch you and you fell off the trolley and hit your head on the side." James shrugs and lights his roll-up. As usual, he shows no signs of interest when I try to get him to remember. It's no more interesting to him than the football results - a sport he detests. "Have you seen Martin because he mentioned he had an interview for you with the doctor?" I ask, changing the subject.

"That shit, no, no, man… that man has to go up. I don't want him here yicketty this and yicketty that. Martin man… I hate… trying to do the most prudential of this and that." He snorts derisively. Martin is his pretty hopeless social worker who looks like he'd come of age in the wrong decade, presenting as he does, like a socialist revolutionary party student from the worst end of the 1970s. He wraps his long multicoloured knotted scarf like Tom Baker's Dr Who, three times around his neck, then into the opening of his duffle coat. He has a hangdog expression that makes you think he was at the heart of the miner's strike. He is obviously terrified of James who, even with his linguistic meanderings, has made it clear he holds him in the utmost contempt. "Yes, I know Martin isn't up to much," I agree. "O.K. I'm going to get on with lunch - salmon, spinach and mashed potato, alright?" James nods. With no teeth from the effects of heroin, I have to make food that is easy for him to eat, but I know I'm up against it time-wise as the effects of the vodka will very soon begin to take over.

By the time I have the meal on the table, James is looking wobbly. "James, come and sit down please. Look, I've made a really nice meal. Come on. I have to leave soon so please let's have this together?" James sighs heavily and waves his newly rolled fag at me. "Just this. I'm just to do this one for the main chance."

"No, James. Have it afterwards. Eat first," I plead. He is losing weight and I am finding rotting food in his fridge every time I come down. Pans burnt and left unwashed, remnants of meals hardly touched piled up on top of one another. He clucks with irritation and carefully places the fag back in the tobacco pouch. He looks annoyed. "It's getting cold. Come on and join me. I don't want to eat alone." He gets up and pulls out the chair. He stares at the plate of food. I ignore him and carry on eating. I'm aware of his knee starting to jiggle under the table. I wish he wouldn't do that. He leans forward. Out of the corner of my eye, I see him pick up his fork. It hovers over the fish. The jiggling increases. His breathing comes heavy. Then suddenly, he stabs the fish and throws the fork down.

"Fucking shit!"

"For God's sake James, don't do that. That's really mean. I made this especially for you."

"Yeah, yeah you yicketty yackety. I don't want shit." He gets up and, seizing the fork, violently stirs the food around the plate so it spins off and splatters onto the table.

"James! James!" I shout, pulling the plate away. "Stop that!" His hand comes up as if he is going to hit me but something reins him in so that the blow turns into a grip as he grabs my shoulder and, bending down, he pushes his face into mine, holding the fork up to my eyes. His face is twisted with anger as he lets rip a torrent of words; words that spill out of him, tumbling and jumping, spraying my face with flecks of spit. My ears start to fill up with the sound of fear; adrenaline pumps, making my heart pound, cutting out his voice.

Everything becomes muffled so I can see his mouth moving but I can't hear what he is saying. His face begins to distort. His mouth opens and closes and, to my horror, I see he has teeth. Teeth! His eyes are changing shape, changing colour, turning from blue to brown as his face lengthens and his hair becomes darker. The dent in his head has gone and I am no longer looking at my brother but I'm staring into the face of... Duncan!

I jump up and step back, my chair overturning, clattering to the floor. Duncan shakes his head and looks at me with a smirk on his face. With a snort, he starts to walk away. "Duncan," I shout. He turns. "You're dead. You can't do this." He laughs, shrugs, then moves off again. I look around for something - anything. The plate of food. I reach out and grab it. "Stop! Stop now!" I yell but he ignores me. "Stop! I said stop!" I lunge towards him, raising the plate up high, I bring it down as hard as I can on his head. I can hear myself screaming, "You're dead. I know you're dead!" He staggers under the impact of the plate which breaks into shards. He rocks back, his hand reaches out for something to steady him but flails helplessly in the air as he crashes to the ground. He doesn't move. I run out to the hall. I try and pull the door open but it's locked. Where are the keys? Where are the bloody keys? "James! James! The keys. I need the keys. We need to get out of here." The noise in my ears is like rushing water. "I need the keys, James!" Why doesn't he answer? Why doesn't he come? I think my heart is going to explode it's pumping so fast.

"Angela! Angela! Help!" It's James's voice.

I freeze. Where is James? Where did he go? What has Duncan done to him?! I edge toward the doorway and peer into the sitting room. James is lying on the floor. His leg is twisted underneath him.

"Hurt. Help me."

"Where is he?" I whisper.

"Please, Angela." He holds his hand out to me. I pause and listen.

"Sssh!" I say, putting my finger to my lips, then cautiously step into the room. I pick up a knife off the table as I move towards the kitchen. Keeping to one side of the doorway, I lean forward. No one is there. I look back at James. "Where is he James? Where did he go?" James shakes his head. I step past him and look in the bedroom. Empty.

"Angela help me!" James sounds like he's crying. I go back in and crouch down beside him.

"What did he do to you?"

"Not Duncan," James mutters. "My leg." I gently ease James's leg out from underneath him. He groans with the pain.

"Keys, James. Where are the keys?"

"Here." He gestures to a chain round his belt. I unclip them. "Don't go, Angela."

"Ssh! I'm just going to check. You keep quiet. If he got in here, he must have had keys." I tiptoe to the front door and very gently turn the key in the lock. I stand still, ear to the door listening for the sound of breathing or any movement that might tell me he is hiding on the other side. Carefully, I open the door and inch forward quickly looking right then left. Nothing. The corridor is as empty and as silent as ever. I breathe a sigh of relief and turn back into the flat, locking the door behind me. "He's gone. We're safe." I help James onto the sofa. "I'm going to make you a cup of tea and you can take some of your painkillers." James nods.

“Vodka help,” he replies, rubbing his leg.

“Alright, you have some of that after the tea.” I wipe away a stray bit of spinach caught in his hair.

It’s nearly dusk outside. There is a blush pink streak across the sky. ‘Red sky at night shepherds delight.’ James leans back on the sofa, eyes closed, one hand clasping the bottle of vodka in his lap. I will go soon. I’ve cleared up the mess. I take a final sip of tea.

Now.

I will go now.

I get up. James opens his eyes.

“Not staying?”

“Can’t. Sorry.” I pick up my bag. “Will you be alright? I’ll call you later, ok?” He doesn’t answer but leans back again, closing his eyes. I reach down and rub him gently on his shoulder. “Sorry.” He opens his eyes and looks up at me.

“I know what you did Angela,” he says fluently. “I've always known.” He closes his eyes again. "I'm glad. Duncan bad, bad man."

Back in the car, I stare out of the window unable to move. I can see myself as a little girl crouching behind the door, her head dropped to her chest, face to the wall. Slowly, she begins to turn. She is holding something in her hands. A brick. She looks up; her expression one of guilt and fear.

Chapter Twenty-Six
CATS

1960S

Twelve years old

I love trains. I like the diddley-dee, diddley-dee, diddly-dee sound they make as they go along. It's really comforting, makes me feel safe. Bully, our cat, is mewing a bit. I've got my hand in the box just to let him know I'm here and that he'll be ok. He'll be so thrilled to see our other cat and our dog Kiffa. I can't wait. I wonder what Mum will say. I won't tell her about Duncan. I won't tell anyone, not even James. In any case, it wasn't my fault.

"Tickets please." The guard slides back the door with a slam, which makes me jump. I give him my ticket. "What you got in there then? A tiger? Hope you got a ticket for him!"

"I didn't know I needed a ticket for him," I reply and the guard laughs.

"Only jokin'!" he says and goes out of the carriage. 'Idiot,' I think, 'worrying me like that.'

Bully is mewing again. I open the top of the box a tiny bit so he can see me. "It's ok Bully, it's ok. You're safe with me now. We'll be home soon I promise." I knew we shouldn't have left him so long when we ran away from Duncan. Poor little chap. I expect he's still frightened after Duncan got hold of him. God, I can hardly bear to think about it. He crept up on us without me knowing. I'd been hiding in the bushes and calling Bully as quietly as I could for what seemed like ages and I was beginning to think that either something terrible had happened to him or he was in the house. I couldn't go in there so I knew I'd have to wait until he came out which could be a long time and I start to think I am going to be there all night. Just as I am beginning to feel a bit desperate 'cos I only had a day's return for the train and I didn't have any more money, I see Bully appear over by the garden shed. I think he must have been living in it 'cos there was a hole in the side and he runs in there when he sees me. He looks very thin. I leave the cardboard box behind and creep over. I open the door ever so gently, calling him all the time and squat down so that I'd be on his level. That's what you should do for cats to make them feel safe. He is crouching up at the back, his eyes all big and frightened. "It's alright Bully," I whisper. "It's me, Angela. I've come to take you home. Don't be scared. Look." I hold out my hand with some of the dried cat food I'd brought. He doesn't move, just sits there all bunched up, staring at me nervously, ready to run off at any minute. Very carefully, I crawl towards him and hold out my hand slowly, slowly and he smells the food. After a moment, he reaches forward and eats some. He starts purring then and he lets me give him a stroke. He eats quite a bit of food and begins to relax so I reach forward and gently pick him up. He doesn't struggle. I hold him close to me, stroking his head and scratching him under the chin, which cats love, and he purrs and purrs so he is almost singing. His little body is so thin. "We didn't mean to leave you behind Bully, but we were in a hurry getting away from Duncan in case he came back and stopped us." I can't help it, but I start crying, really quietly as I don't want to upset him. "I'm so sorry. I really am. It's just - things have been a bit difficult. I'll never leave you again I promise." His fur starts getting wet so I pull myself together. I wipe my nose on my sleeve as I haven't got a hanky. "Right, we must get going." I get up and turn round and, standing in the doorway is Duncan.

God, it gives me a shock.

I gasp and sort of jump, which makes Bully stick his claws into me, which is quite painful. "Come to get the cat, Angela? Don't you think it would have been polite to ring and ask first before you turn up? That's what normal people do. Where's your mother?"

"She's not here."

"Don't start that again. Is she hiding somewhere in the car? Is that it?"

"No." I shake my head. "She's not here."

He looks like he's going to have a brainstorm. He starts sort of puffing and grimacing and shaking his head. "You know, if it hadn't been for you children," he sneers, glaring at me. "Your mother and I would still be together. You wrecked our marriage." Suddenly, he lunges towards me and tears the cat out of my arms. Bully yowls. He has him by the scruff and is dangling him in front of me. You should never hold an older cat by its scruff as they're too heavy and it hurts them.

I shout at him, "She's not here, she's not here. Give him back, you're hurting him." But he turns away and marches off.

"Just tell me where she is Angela, then you can have your cat back." He walks on, swinging Bully out to one side.

I run after him but I don't know what to do to stop him and I'm crying and yelling at the same time, "I'm telling the truth, she's not here, she's not here." He takes no notice. "Stop! Stop!" I shout, but he just goes on walking, goes on ignoring me, walking away with Bully.

So that's when I do it. I look around for something to stop him and I see the brick. I pick it up and hit him hard on the back of the head. I have to. The first time I hit him he stumbles and cries out, but he keeps holding onto Bully so the second time I bring it down harder with both hands. This time he drops to the ground letting go of Bully. I manage to grab Bully before he gets away and I run over to the cardboard box. I'm all fingers and thumbs trying to get him in and he's clawing and growling and I'm shaking and I'm panicking so I can't tie the string properly because I think Duncan will be after me but, when I start to run off down the drive, I look back over my shoulder and I can see the back of his body lying on the ground. He isn't moving.

Bully has calmed right down now. He's got his eyes closed and his paws tucked under him. My hand is resting on his little neck so my thumb can just rub him gently under his chin. I'm beginning to recognise the countryside outside, so we aren't far from home.

I'll tell you about the white kitten now. Remember, I told Maggie I couldn't? Well, I can now.

The white kitten lay on the blue velvet curtain. It was dark in the house. Mummy hadn't come home again, so we were waiting for her. The kitten kept crying. I found him some milk and gave it to him but, every time he lapped it up, he was sick. I didn't understand why. He kept looking at me and mewing and I stroked him and he purred and I told him that, when Mummy came home, she would make him better. But she didn't come home. Instead, the old lady from the school came and she told us she was taking us back with her. I refused to go because I had to wait for her to come back and save my sick kitten.

“Don’t be silly Angela,” the old lady said and she just gave my kitten this look like he was dirty or something and yanked me out the door. At four years old, I didn’t have the strength to stop her.

The kitten died in the night.

I should have saved him, but I couldn’t and it’s hurt me ever since.

Today makes things a bit better because today I saved Bully.

I saved him.

And he will never be unsaved.

Never,

ever,

ever.

EPILOGUE

Four weeks ago, I lay alone in a tribal hut designated solely for women. Outside, the African women sang up the songs of their ancestors, those who had gone before; mothers, fathers, grandmothers, aunts, perhaps even sons and daughters. The songs were sung to keep the lives of the disappeared still present, to bring comfort to themselves as they sat swaying next to one another, releasing the words, expressing their love out into the darkness.

I had no song for my mother or James. If I had, it would have come out as a strangled croak.

It had been 2 years since James died. He got sepsis and had to have his leg amputated. The home I had got him into was only a little better than the flat (which he almost set on fire a couple of times) but I think it was just a question of time. He had stopped drinking after the amputation but continued to smoke. Then, an inmate returned from a day out with Covid and that did for him. On Christmas day, he died. I believe he wanted to go, maybe he had been for a long time, and I couldn't blame him. It was no life.

The weight of loss I lugged around with me was like a huge sponge pressing on my lungs, getting heavier each day, as it absorbed the inexhaustible tears.

I'd been living in a world of virtual reality, experiencing life because I was alive but not living. I could only appreciate the wonder of the world through an objective lens, but I couldn't feel it because all the feelings I had were absorbed into a morass of sadness.

I made a decision. I applied for several credit cards, which they gave to people like free sweeties, and bought myself a ticket to Southern Africa. I had always wanted to go there and my plan was to backpack around, go wherever it took me, stay in hostels and, once done, I could go home, shoot myself, shoot my horse (as I didn't trust anyone to look after her) and thus put an end to my narrative.

Kayaking down the Orange River in Namibia, the heat is intense. No breeze to ruffle it. In the stillness of the afternoon, the dip and pull of the paddles are the only sound. The paddling goes on and on. I feel like my arms are going to fall off. We glide through a terrain of desert sand that remains the same mile after mile, only punctuated now and again by huge mountains of shale. There is a ribbon of patchy green, like a lampshade braid, along the edge of the river with the occasional bent willow and spiky scrub struggling to hold onto the bank.

As we break to set up camp, we see an ebony black merman fishing for his tribe. He rises out of the water like some mythical creature - a Namibian Neptune - the water rolling off his polished body gleaming in the sun. Miles from anywhere, his task is a solitary one. Days of fishing and catching and drying, alone with no human contact, I wonder where his thoughts went.

The sun slides down behind the rim of the horizon. The campfire is dowsed. The quiet of the desert wraps around us travellers.

Lying in my sleeping bag on the bank of the river, I'm transfixed by the appearance of the stars as they softly materialise, their brightness sharpening with the darkening sky. The glittering trail of the Milky Way, as if cast carelessly like seeds from the hand of some divine goddess, scintillates above. There is the little red dot of Mars emerging. This is the opening of a celestial extravaganza, the first act before the moon begins its ascendance, flooding the night sky with a bone-white light, dimming each constellation with its radiance. Like a prima ballerina, it gradually assumes its place centre stage as the corp de ballet of stars melts into shadow.

The light of the moon casts strange features onto the huge shale mountain rising up on the opposite side of the river. As my gaze rests there, it seems to take on some kind of human form. I'm staring at what appears to be the monstrous head of some pitiless giant, reminiscent of Ozymandias. Unlike Ozymandias, this giant, with its lower body buried deep in the sand, gives me a worrying sense that it is alive. The face has a cruel expression and seems to be looking down upon me, a hostile trespasser. I turn my head slowly to see if any of my fellow travellers are awake, but no one stirs. I glance back at the mountain giant. Is it my imagination but has it moved closer? What if it were to free the rest of its body imprisoned in the sand? I can see it lumbering towards me, reaching down to pluck me off the ground and crush me in its massive stone-carved hands, or worse still, eat me. Maybe that would be all too good; maybe this messenger of nature, eyeing me with malevolence, reinforces what I already suspect, that I am loathsome to the world for what I have done. Is this my retribution?

As if out of nowhere, the words of a poem come into my mind; a part of a passage I had to learn at school.

'... a huge cliff,
As if voluntary power instinct,
Upreared its head
'And, growing still in stature, the huge cliff
Rose up between me and the stars, and still,
With measured motion, like a living thing

Strode after me.'

Wordsworth in the Lake District. Rowing a boat across a black lake on a still, moonlit night. How strange that this has surfaced from nowhere. I remember thinking how frightening it must have been and here it is with me, years later, precisely echoing my feelings of fear and dread. The words run round and round in my head, my terror growing; irrational but real. Unlike Wordsworth, I cannot run. I'm in the middle of the Namibian desert. I sit up and look again at the other sleeping bags. Nothing reassuring there. If the monster moves, they will be squashed to death under its solid stone feet, their body parts squiggling up like minced meat between its toes. I wriggle back down into my bag and listen to my heart pounding away. The interior becomes slick with sweat. I try to keep as still as possible in case I catch the monster's eye. The fear is overwhelming. I cannot quieten it. There is no chair to push up against a door, no mother waiting downstairs, no god to pray to. Will I hear the thing levering itself up out of the ground? Will the earth shake with the force of its thudding footfall as it strides towards me? Terror reaches a fever pitch but there is nowhere for it to go unless I combust or have a heart attack. Then, the fear plateaus, mutates and turns in on itself. Slowly, slowly, it drains away, as a new thought pushes itself to the fore. Something different, something once known begins to take shape in my mind. Is it possible that the shale mountain, the moon, the desert and myself are all one, all elements of nature? Isn't that what I once believed? I hear James's voice, "We're from the stars, Ange. We're all made of carbon, just a matter of atoms, crowding together." I peep out cautiously from undercover. My heartbeat slows. I sit up. The shale mountain is just a shale mountain. My eyes search the heavens once more and glimpse behind the veil of the moon's glow, half seen, other stars, other life, blinking quietly back in the dark. The beauty of nature that I am a part of; the beauty and the power that had disappeared and which I had forgotten. Gradually light and hope filter through. Sitting on the desert floor illuminated by the moon, the crushing alienation of the years begins to dissolve.

I let out an exhausted sigh as all the tension seeps out of my body. Another feeling slips tentatively into its place. It's quite ordinary. Not ecstatic, not optimistic, it's just... alright.

I feel alright.

Alright is enough.

Just enough to carry on.

END